A Concise

D1633480

Scotland From

Day One to Day Two

by

Davytheghost

To Mark
Enjoy!!

Davytheghost.

Published by Aultbea Publishing, Inverness

Copyright details

Davytheghost
A concise history of Scotland from Day One to Day Two

First published in Great Britain by
Aultbea Publishing Company in 2005,
28 Church Street, Inverness IV1 1HB

Second Edition

ISBN 0-9549340-5-9

£9.95

Printed by Highland Printers Limited
Henderson Road, Inverness IV1 1SP

This book is dedicated to Lucy Morrison, even though she as relentlessly pursued by her slave driver of a boss – Roy. Also to my mother and father, whose humour influenced this book.

A Concise History of Scotland From Day One to Day Two

To begin at the beginning, which is the best place to start, God (also known as the boss) made the earth. While making it he said to Adam (also known as number one son), 'here I will place Scotland, it will be a great land with beautiful hills and great Lochs. I will give it the best wildlife, a fantastic place and I am going to make the people the most intelligent and the bravest in the world.' At this point Adam said to God,'hey boss why are you being so kind to this race.' To which God replied, 'wait till you see who I am giving them for neighbours.' So begins the history of Scotland...

To start with Scotland was very much like any other place, not much there and bugger all to do on a Saturday night. The Scots come from mostly a mixed group of mongrels. Twelve thousand years ago bonnie Scotland was not so flaming bonnie! In fact it was cold enough to freeze the balls off a brass caveman! Scotland was covered in big lumps of ice - and not the kind ye stick in yer whisky either. This of course was the last in a series of ice ages. Which came first the ice or the locals? That's a good question, no one knows for sure. In England, (known these days as over the wall) remains have been found dating back over 200,000 years (from about the time England last won the World Cup!). Nothing has yet been found in Scotland dating this far back (except an old black and white video of the 1966 World Cup). This does not mean early man never came this far north, all it means is that they were clever chappies and cleaned up their shite after them. Any evidence these dudes might have left behind has been destroyed.

In 8000BC the ice became water and shaped the land that we see before us today. With the big ice cubes no more; Scotland became the 'in' place to be. Animals started to live in the newly formed land. As the weather started to get less Baltic, the first known settlers made their way here. It's also about this time that the English invented the wheel. Thankfully the Scots made it round! Man (and the odd woman) had made his way to bonnie Scotland. These chappies came from places that were lucky enough not to have been under the big chunks of ice. In those grand old days there were of course no fish n' chip shops. This meant that the new guys on the block had to be hunters. If you were going to eat, you had to catch yer own grub!

The oldest discovered settlement dates back to 6500BC. This period of time is known by the lovely name of the Mesolithic period. These guys started to get their act together, fishing and hunting being the big thing of the day. They started to settle all over Scotland, living mostly near trees and water. They would drink the water and piss on the trees.

They led very basic simple lives; they didn't have all the mod cons that were to follow later. Things like stone forts or clay pots; they didn't even have metal tools for hitting each other over the nut with. Having said that, these guys were really clued up on how to get the most from the land.

For digs they lived in tent-like dwellings built around poles, these were classy joints with brushwood and animal skins for covering, a thing that the animals themselves weren't overly chuffed about. People in those far off days weren't midgets as most people think, in fact the average height of a man chappie was 5ft 7in and the women were 5ft 3in. Also in those days one could expect to live to the ripe old age of 10 to 25 years. It's also a good guess to say these guys didn't go about in the raw. Scotland being a little chilly round the willy makes this very unlikely. It's not known what they wore, but a good guess would be that animal hides were the fashion of the day. As for grub there was a good supply of wild animals; from bears to wild cattle, to be killed and noshed. If you had a bad day hunting you could always go home and cook the wife! This simple casual way of life carried on for the next three to four thousand years.

In or about 4000BC came some farming chappies, we now have the arrival of the Neolithic farmers (Neolithic man can still be found in certain pubs in Glasgow). This is when Stone Age man really started to get his act together. Neolithic chappie created a mode of existence, with everyday things like housing and sowing the land. To make it easier to get their hands on grub they kept livestock. In those far off days getting into Scotland was a pain. The terrain was as rough as a badger's arse with very dense forests and boggy moorlands. The guys who did make their way to settle here came by boat. All this of course is very nice but where did the Scots come from? The Scots are basically a Celtic race. The Celts migrated from Central Europe. Some came directly from the mainland, while others staggered through what is now France and Spain. When one remembers there were no trains in those days, this seems a bloody stupid thing to do, as it was one heck of a walk (at this stage one thinks that maybe drink had something to do with the migration). These guys all spoke a different lingo, but left us no written word. All we know of these dudes today come from archaeologists and linguists. The Celts were kind enough to leave us many whopping big standing stones!

There have been many suggestions what these stones stood for, but no one knows for sure. It could be that the stones were a way of communicating to other tribes. Or it well may be the case that they stood for sod all, and were put up by the Celts knowing full well that it would confuse the living daylights out of us for thousands of years! One thing we do know about the Celts is that they came from Central Europe. Roughly where Austria and Switzerland is now. Remains of their boats have been found containing cork from where these counties are now. The Celts were not a group of guys you would want to fall out with on a Saturday night. They were a warrior race, enjoying a good punch-up.

Truth is they were a tough lot.

They reached the top of their power ladder in the fourth century BC. Their main claim to fame is that they once booted the Romans up the hole. They overran Rome; no mean feat in those days. After the Celts kicked the Roman backsides the Romans knew them as fearless warriors. This was most likely due to the fact that some of them, the Gaesatue, were so contemptuous of life that they actually fought in the scud (Scottish for naked)!

According to Julius Caesar (also known as Big Brute to his mates) the Roman chappie that invaded England (with a little help from his army), the Celts were deeply religious. This is interesting as they were also Pantheists who worshipped the sun and the stars and even sheepshit. For entertainment they believed in human sacrifice. They kept slaves and collected the heads of their enemies (a bit like your modern day football fan). The Celts were also very clever bunnies and their artists produced some of the most interactive design work ever created. Luck was running out for them, and things like inferior metal

technology ensured that they were soon becoming the back runners. They could no longer match the weapons or the discipline of the big bad Romans. This meant the Celts ended up getting their own rear ends kicked. The Romans now being the big boys decided to conquer the world and why not. They took England without too many problems. Mr Caesar being a sensible chappie decided not to be a silly boy and try to invade bonnie Scotland. Besides there was nothing worth nicking.

To be fair to the Roman dudes they had their work cut out with England and Wales. It was 37 years before the Romans set their yaks on Scotland. By this time they were led by a chappie who went by the girls blouse name of Julius Argricola (take the 'Argri' away and we have the world's first recorded Cola). The year old Cola Face came to Scotland was AD 80.

The Roman legions slogged their way over the Cheviot Hills into the land they called 'Caledonia,' putting up a few forts on the way. This was their name for what we now call Scotland. Taking the Lowlands wasn't much of a problem for Mr Argricola and his mates. He had a series of forts built in order to launch his invasion of the North. He found himself some cosy digs in Stirling and this brings us on to the first recorded major punch-up on Scottish soil, the scrap of 'Mons Graupius.

It is from this period the first named Scot appears. Roman historians left us written word of him. If they were not telling porkies and they may well have been, his name was Cagacus. A geezer with a name like a smelly plant. He was the boss of a gang of guys called the 'Caledonii.'

The Romans were to come face to face with this mob at the battle of 'Mons Graupius and being the victors, they left written word to say that as well as giving the 'Caledonii' a good trashing they also left many thousands dead. Among the many natives who copped their lot was Mr Cagacus. He no longer held the jobbie as leader of the 'Caledonians as he was deed (and that's Scottish for dead).

As to where this battle took place no one really has a flaming clue. Some stab a guess that it was the hill of Moncreiffe, but there's no real proof. Since we're clueless as to where the fight took place, we have named a whole region after it; The Grampians.

At this stage things were looking pretty good for the Roman dudes. In the summer of 83 Agricola having spent the winter on the banks of the Tay, said to his mate 'Dee' I'm 'Dun' with this place (and that became Dundee) and decided to continue his invasion of the North. About this time that big guy called fate stuck his oar in, Agricola was recalled to sunny Rome. This was all but the end of the Roman conquest of Scotland. They did stick their noses in now and again but it was more a defensive action than an offensive one. This of course means that Scotland was only minimally Romanized. In 121 (good chat up line that one) the Roman Emperor, a big shot by the name of Hadrian, came to have a wee look for himself. He soon put his plan into action and built a big wall from Solway to the Tyne.

About 20 years after that another Roman chappie by the ridiculous name of Lollius Urbicus built another wall this time from the Forth to the Clyde. It became known as the Antonine wall. Fed up getting their faces punched by the locals the Romans soon jacked this wall in and moved back to the safety of Hadrian's wall.

They left much written about the locals, the northern tribes. It is from here that we first hear of the Picts. The Romans being sharp and on the ball, soon noticed all the local warriors had one thing in common; the lot of them were covered in tattoos. This is where the name Picts comes from... Pictorial.

The land the Romans failed to conquer was basically a desert with nothing worth stealing. To the chappies the Romans called the Picts this was their 'nothing' and they would fight like hell for that nothing. It might be nothing to anyone else but this nothing was their home. It was the Picts' ability to put up a good fight that pissed the Romans off. The Picts would march right into the ranks of the Romans, cracking many a skull on the way. They would fight like nutters, and then suddenly they would stop. They would move back, the Romans would feel great thinking they had won. Then in the distance they would notice the Picts jumping up and down like loonies.

At this stage the Romans thought the Pict chappies had lost the plot and had gone completely off their trolleys. The Romans would stand and have a good laugh at them. What they had failed to notice was the Picts were jumping up and down on their swords. This was to straighten out the metal, which had got bent during the fighting. Once the metal was straight again right back into the thick of it they would go. The Romans were the first to find the Scots didn't have much time for invaders.

About the year 430 the Romans started to drift away leaving the locals to do their own thing. To be honest this in fact didn't do the inhabitants any great favours. The reason is simple because it left them to the mercy of their nasty neighbours.

At this time Scotland had four races. The hardest were the Picts who ruled from Caithness in the North to the Forth in the South, they were of course from good Celtic stock. Next to them were the Britons of Strathclyde; they were also of Celtic stock. These guys were the boss men from the Clyde to the Solway right on to Cumbria. In the East, south of the Forth was controlled by the Teutonic/Saxons their land stretched all the way to Northumbria.

More importantly, to the west lay the Kingdom of Dalriada. This land was ruled by a Celtic bunch of guys called the Scotees who had made their way over from Ireland. These war-mongering dudes were led by a guy called Feargus Mor (also known as 'Big Fergie' to his mates).

It is from this bunch of Irish rejects that the name Scots comes from. Somewhere along the line the 'ee' has been dropped. The Scotees moved up the Great Glen (I'll bet they did) introducing themselves to the locals, then kicking the shit out of them. It is about this time that the most fundamental event in Scottish history happened (no the Scottish football team didn't actually score a goal). It was 'The coming of St Columba.' Rude as this may sound Columba's arrival was to change the face of Scottish history forever. For with him, he brought a small thing called Christianity. Having had his arse booted out off Ireland for murdering a few hundred people he came here in peace. Columba came to Scotland to bring the Holy News. He was not a bloke going about selling newspapers with holes in them, but a warrior who went around converting people. He most likely gave you a choice, believe in God or I'll nut you. Not surprisingly, most converted. Big Boy came here in 563 and there are many tales of his epic struggles.

One such tale is his arrival to Inverness in 565. He made his way to the town because he wanted to convert the Pictish King Brude to Christianity. Brudes fort was on the other side of the river Ness. To get there he would have to swim over. He was about to do this when one of the locals came running out and said to him 'here boy if you go in that water a dirty great beastie will come up and eat you.' Mr Columba being a brave man sent another man in the water and told him to swim to the other side. Sure enough as the man got half way across the water, up raised a huge monster. The poor man in the water was no doubt filling his breeks (that's Scottish for trousers) when Columba rushed forward and held up his crucifix. He then said in the nice sweet voice of a saint 'go away you nasty beast and don't come back.' Columba blessed the monster and told it to go away at great speed and not to bother eating anyone again. The monster did go away but it didn't go very far, in fact only four miles up the river to Loch Ness! It has been there for the last 1500 years and should be due its pension soon, but the good thing is it hasn't eaten anyone since Columba gave it a ticking off! Having dealt with the monster, Columba made his way across the water and up the hill to the fort of King Brude. On his arrival there he discovered the fort had big wooded doors with large iron bolts holding them closed. Columba knocked on the door, there was no answer, Brude was a Pagan and happy to be so. Columba knocked again but still no answer, perhaps Brude thought it was a Jehovah's Witness at the door. Brude was not going to answer the door. So Columba stepped back and held up his crucifix suddenly a ray light came from the sky and the bolts flew from the doors. He walked in followed by the ray of light. Brude soon decided he wasn't going to argue with any dude that was a dab hand at the old miracle game. He was soon converted to Christianity. Columba gets most of the credit for bringing Christianity to Scotland. This however is not entirely fair as there were other dudes involved in this game as well. St Ayden and St Ninian to name but two.

As the years went on Scotland was fast becoming a Christian country. Before a country can become a country it needs three things. A King, a flag and a patron saint. A King was no problem we had loads of them. A flag no problem any twat can draw a flag. A patron saint, now that was a problem, we didn't have one, so how could we get one. This little problem was solved one starry night when a wandering mystic wandered into the camp of one of the Kings of Dalriada. In some of his luggage he just happed to have with him a bag of bones. He soon got chatting to the King and told him the bones were of a dude called St Andrew. For some unknown reason, most likely over a few drams, the King took this hook line and sinker! So a fisherman who never set foot in Scotland became our patron saint.

There is another version of how St Andy got the jobbie. In the 8th century a chappie who went by the name of St Rule was given charge of Andy's relics. He was having a snooze one night when an angel told him in a dream 'go to Scotland laddie for a wee holiday and take Andy's bones with you.' Not being one to argue with guys with big wings, he set off for bonnie Scotland. He arrived in what is now known as St Andrews. He got on well with the locals and built a church, where of course he took on the jobbie as its first Bishop. Who was this dude St Andrew anyway, he had friends in high places, as he was one of Jesus' mates. He taught the gospel in some joints called Scythia, Epirus and Achaia. Being a clever dude he also preached from the cross to a wee group of people roughly 20,000 just before he crocked it. Not only is he our patron saint, he also holds the same jobbie in Russia. While we're on about patron saints, it's worth noting how Ireland got their patron saint, Saint Patrick. Paddy was born on the West Coast of Scotland. Not paying much attention to what he was doing one day, he was smacked over the nut and taken to Ireland as a slave. He didn't like being a slave much, so he worked his way up to the rank of patron saint.

This of course means St Paddy is in fact a Scot! From the year 800 Scotland had an influx of visitors some dudes called Vikings. For a start these big sea-warriors never wore horns in their hats! This was dreamed up by Hollywood hundreds of years later. To start the story of the Vikings we go to a lump of rock now called the Isle of Iona. It was on this lump of rock that Columba had founded a monastery in 563. Business was doing no too bad and it had been getting better for two centuries by the visiting Scottish, Pictish, Northern British and Anglo-Saxon Kings.

All this of course meant Iona was the 'in' place of cultural and religious ways of the day and it was therefore the number one target for the nasty smelly chappies from Scandinavia. Iona was a remote, middle of nowhere, lump of rock and that suited the Celtic monks and hermits of the day just grand. Its remoteness left it wide open for attack from the sea. It was therefore one of the first victims of the big bearded baddies.

It was first attacked in 795 and the Vikings enjoyed themselves so much they came back in 802. In 806 they came again, this time with an attitude and showing what bad eggs they were. They landed, had a wee look at the scenery then done in 68 of the monks. In 807 it was decided by the monks that this was no funny so they all buggered off and moved their monastery (they must have been big guys it's no easy carrying a monastery) to Kells in Ireland.

Not all crapped themselves, some decided to stay and face the wrath of the big bad chappies from the land of the freezing. The monk's boss was a Paddy who went by the name of Blathmac (also known as 'Have a Bath Mac' to his mates). He was taking no shit and stood his ground. The Vikings being an understanding lot made a deal with him. They told him he could stay with his buddies. There was however one small condition attached; he had to tell them were St Columba's shrine was hidden. Blathmac told them to get stuffed, not his brightest idea as this well and truly pissed off the Vikings. They kicked the living shit out of him, then for good measure they ripped the poor guy to pieces. Being an understanding chappie he put this down as having a bad day!

Why did the smelly hippie look-a-like Vikings want Iona so much? Truth is they couldn't give a monkey's toss about a small windswept lump of rock. However they did have expensive tastes without having to pay. Iona was the 'in' place for the real McCoy, beautiful bits of odds and ends made of gold and silver. Thus the Vikings were attracted to the peaceful little Isle to conduct business. You know, the usual haggling; they would cut a few throats cut a few heads off and take whatever they flaming well wanted. These guys were also after another kind of loot, they were avid collectors of slaves. Slaves had two uses; one, they could be taken back to the land of the frozen dinners and put to work, or they could be sold at markets in the Muslim world. There the lucky slave would fetch good dosh for his master.

Mr & Mrs Viking liked Scotland so much that they started to move over in great numbers. The reason is unclear, but most likely for economic reasons. One thing about these dudes is that they were dab hands at building boats. In fact they were so chuffed with them; some of the Vikings had their boats buried with them! The less said about that the better. The Vikings were about as popular as a porcupine on a waterbed. There are many accounts of battles with Scottish Kings. The big moth-eaten gits were a pain in the backside and something had to be done. One of the ancient Kings of Scotland had a brainwave. He told the geezers with the smelly hairy armpits that anything they could sail a long ship round was theirs to keep! The Viking King said 'aye yer on mate.' Thus the Vikings sailed their ships round every one of the hundreds of islands off the coast of Scotland, making them their property. The Scottish Kings keeping control of most of the mainland. The bullyboy's from Norway and Denmark were indeed nasty bad eggs to anyone who got in their face. They were not all bad eggs however and some of them were quite cool dudes and formed peaceful settlements. Big and hairy they may have been but they also considered themselves as poets;

> 'On a hill there stood a man
> I said you're a pain
> So now he's slain'

They also had a liking for works of art and they certainly had their own way of acquiring them! It was in those so-called peace camps that amazingly the first form of political democracy was first introduced into Britain. This came about after the rotten core of the big greasy chappies had been chased off from the isles in the middle of the 9th century. A district magistrate who was known by the lovely title of 'Great Foude' was sent around the settlements to administer Norse Odal Law. This law was based on Dude Olaf's 'Book of Laws.' It was the Great Foudes jobbie to hold an annual supreme court, which was called a 'Thing.' At these get togethers all freemen had to attend and take part in the goings on. There was fun to be had by all as new laws were dished out. Most enjoyable, anyone who had stepped out of line would have their wrists well and truly slapped. Every decision had to be taken by the majority of all present i.e. 'all in favour of poking big yaks in the eye raise yer hand.' The 'Thing' was the main man, but under the 'Thing' there was lots of lower 'Things.' The jobbies of these district courts, which were headed by not so great Foudes, was to deal with the minor goings on. These Foudes employed chappies known as 'Ranselmen' and it was their job to do all the everyday jobbies like spying on their fellow neighbours. They also had the pleasant task of going to other people's homes and say 'hello what a nice day', have a cup of tea then check their houses for any nicked gear. Every settlement also had a chappie called a 'Lawrightman' this dude didn't have too many mates, as he was the guy who worked out how much tax you owed. They stayed in Scotland till Alexander III kicked their hairy arse's back to where they came from in the first place! Of course by this time the damage was done. The Norse language had been absorbed into the population. Indeed to this day many words spoken in Scotland are in fact Norse i.e. Kirk (church).

The Vikings were only one of a number of things going on in the 9th century. In 843 Kenneth MacAlpien (also known as 'Smarty Pants' to his mates) became King of Alban, Scotland. Here starts the story of the Kings of Alba. Kenny had done the near impossible and succeeded in uniting the Scottish Picts. This made Kenny the main dude of the day. Maybe old Kenny was in the right place at the right time. The story of the Kings of Alba is not as straightforward as one may think. Big Ken was a Gael, he was a descendant of Fergus who came over from Dalriada in Ireland to form the Kingdom of Dalriada in Scotland. One old tale tells of how Kenny got to the height of his power. He invited all the Pictish big cheeses round for a meal at his joint. He really laid on the works and had a giant spread prepared. The big boys stuffed their greedy faces until they couldn't move from the table. At this point bolts were released from under their seats and they were all thrown into a pit below. For desert Kenny had them all slaughtered. How Kenny really got to the top is not known but get there he did. He was a classy guy who worked his way to the top. It is known that the 'Gaelicisation' of the Picts was well under way well before Mr MacAlpien came along. In 858 Big Ken gave up the jobbie and died. Over the next few years the Kings were known as the Kings of Alba. At this time Alba only included the land north of the Forth-Clyde. Strathclyde and the Lowlands were ruled by the Britons and Angles, the new Kingdom Gaelic. This was a violent time in Scottish history. The Kings had their hands full with baddies from the land of frostbite. The turning point at this time was by the reign of Mr MacAlpien's grandson.

Constantine (also known as 'Con-Artist' to his mates) in those hard days ruled for an incredible 43 years. This is an almost unbelievable achievement for those days. Even then, old Constantine didn't die a violent death, he simply retired to Culdee Monastery in St Andrews. Other than the length of his reign and his peaceful demise not a heck of a lot is known of Constantine's reign. What is known is he was determined to push his boundaries southwards. His main pain was the Scandinavian sea Kings from the dynasty of 'Hy-Ivarr.' There is no doubt that Con Artist was really pissed off with the 'Hy-Ivarr.' He spent the first 20 years of his reign kicking their heads in. He also gave a lending hand to the beleaguered English in the north who were having a hard time with the 'Hy-Ivarr.' In 921 he got into a pact with some of his pals and acknowledged Edward the Elder. Having made a few chums it was time for one hell of a punch-up. The year was 937 and the fight was to be at Brunanburh. Constantine most likely wished he'd stayed in bed that morning as the battle was a complete fuck-up. His army was destroyed. Nevertheless,

Con Artist's reign was one of success as he greatly reduced the threat from the Vikings. He also moved his authority into the south of Scotland. Constantine stopped breathing in 943; his successors didn't quite get the knack of things.

He was followed by Malcolm I who lasted for 11 years 'til the daft git got himself killed. In fact the next few Kings had a nasty habit of getting themselves killed in battle. At this point we move on to Duncan who reigned from 1034-1040 until he copped his lot from Macbeth. First of all, let's not get confused with Macbeth (also known as 'Don't Say That Bloody Name To Me' by his mates) There are two Macbeths, one King of Scotland, the other a play by an English dude called Wullie Shakespeare. The two are as different as chalk and cheese. To start with, Duncan, who Macbeth butchered, was not a frail old chappie, but a young dude in his late 20's. What kind of King was Macbeth? He was in fact a dab hand at the jobbie. After doing Duncan in he took the throne for himself and his wife; who was called Mrs Macbeth. The easiest way to tell the story of Macbeth or as he would have been called in Gaelic 'Maelbeatha', is to compare the history with that of Mr Shakespeare. To start with the play says that Macbeth with some mates; killed Duncan in Inverness. This is not the least bit likely. Duncan was probably killed in or near Elgin. Mr Shake Rattle and Roll also says Mrs Macbeth had her hand in Duncan's demise; more doo-dah dreamed up by old shaky face.

In real life Mrs Macbeth was a loyal wife who stood by her man. She also had the adorable first name of Gruach! Indeed before she got hitched to Mr Macbeth she had been hitched before and had a son who went by the silly name of 'Lulach.' Such was the respect he held that he was known as the 'Fool.' Macbeth thought Lulach was the bees-knees; in fact he was crowned King after Macbeth. Mr Shakespeare also gibbers on about Macbeth 'doing in' Banquo. We can be fairly sure that he didn't kill Mr Banquo owing to one small fact, the bugger never existed. He was merely a figment of imagination. Another chappie in Mr Shake-Rattle-and-Roll's play is MacDuff who is said to have slain Macbeth, more bull-shit. MacDuff, having the same thing in common with Banquo, also never existed. Having said all that, Shakespeare's play is a very enjoyable account of Macbeth's history, but must never be confused with the real facts. The fact is Macbeth was indeed a strong and able leader.

In 1050 he even went on a wee holiday to Rome. (Maybe he got one of those mega bus deals for a quid). When he got there, he scattered his dosh among the poor like seed, (this dude can visit me anytime), thus was the custom for a ceremonial entry into Rome.Why he went to Rome is unclear; but it would be for one of two reasons. He may well have gone on a Pilgrimage; or he might have gone to see what the big boys in Rome could do for Scotland. Or maybe he just fancied a good cheesy pizza! In those days Scotland was still a backward country. The fact that Macbeth was able to go to the land of pasta and return to his Kingdom intact speaks for itself. However, seven years later Duncan's oldest offspring bore a little bit of a grudge about Macbeth killing his papa. So he met up with Macbeth, nutted him, then hit him a right sore one with his sword so Macbeth ended up very much dead, thus Duncan returned his father's throne to the family.Being fair chuffed with himself, he was crowned Malcolm III or as he was called in his day 'Ceann Mor' which translates as 'Big Head' (there's quite a few of them in my bar I can tell ya).

To start the story of 'Big Head', we go back to the year 1054. It was the year that the 23 year old Malcolm came back to Scotland after spending 14 years in England, (poor sod). He came back with a mate of his, an English dude who went by the name of Earl of Siward. For good measure they brought with them an army.

He met up with Macbeth at Lothian, said hello, then kicked his backside out of town. Three years later they bumped into each other again at a place called Lumphanan. It was here that Macbeth found out just how pissed off Malcolm was.

Malcolm killed Macbeth, but before he could go around calling himself King he had the slight problem of Macbeth's stepson with the silly name. He met up with him for a wee chinwag. Lulach being the fool he was, let Malcolm stick a sword right through him! Lulach of course fell to the ground and died.

Malcolm was crowned King on 25th April 1058. But before we continue though, we must 'fast forward' 8 years to the Norman Conquest of England. This of course changed the history of Britain forever. The year was 1066 and the result: Normans 1 England 0. England had once again been stuffed, this time by a group of Froggies.

Harold the English King was killed. Now it is just possible that before the battle of Hastings, King Harold was out inspecting his troops. He went up to the first soldier who was carrying a spear and said; 'tell me my good man what you can do with that?' The soldier replied, 'Sir, see that eagle a mile above?' 'Yes,' said the King. At this stage the soldier threw his spear up into the air and right through the eagle. The King being fair impressed moved on to the next dude who had a mace. King Harold asked what he could do with it, the soldier replied 'Sir, see that cow on the hill two miles away?' 'Yes,' said the King. 'Well Sir, just you watch this,' replied the soldier. At this stage he began to swing the mace then threw it, hitting the cow and killing it. The King, now feeling very chuffed, moved on to the next soldier who had a bow and arrow. Harold asked him what he could do. The soldier replied, 'Sir, see that barn door 6 feet away?' 'Yes,' said the King. 'Well Sir watch this.' At this stage the soldier fired his arrow and missed the barn door by 80 feet! 'Watch him, he'll have some bugger's eye out with that thing,' Harold whispered to one of his Generals. As luck would have it, Harold copped his lot at the battle of Hastings with an arrow in his yak. After the Battle of Hastings in which the English came a poor second, there were many who fled to Scotland. These were dudes who didn't fancy getting their nuts kicked by the Normans, so they came to bonnie Scotland for safety.

Among these refugees was a dude by the dreadful name of Edgar the Atheling (one can only assume that his Mum and Dad had a good sense of humor when they gave him that name). Edgar's claim to fame was that he was claimant to the English throne, which had been nicked by a bunch of smelly Normans. With him he brought his sister Margaret. This wee lass was born in Hungary and raised over the wall in the English Court of Edward the Confessor ('Admit to Nothing', that's my motto). Meanwhile Malcolm was getting too big for his boots, thinking of ideas of how to expand his Kingdom. So in 1070 he set about this by doing two things. First of all he achieved a minor thing, he invaded England. Secondly, he got his claws into Margaret and got hitched to her. All this achieved something else... it made him as popular as a hole in the head with William the Conqueror.

William was now very pissed off with Malky and saw him as one cheeky git, who was a threat to his rule over England. In 1072 William repaid Malcolm the favour and invaded Scotland.

At Abernethy, Malcolm met up with William and knew he had to do some fast-talking or he was 'out the window'. So he said sorry for being a prick, promising not to do anything that might upset William again. William listened to what Malcolm had to say for himself then said, 'fine, but don't let it happen again or else.'

King Malcolm and Queen Margaret were an odd couple to say the least. Maggie was half the age of Malcolm and his main interests were causing trouble and killing people. Her main interests were helping the poor and needy. When she married the King, he was a bit of a rough diamond but she was determined to sort him out. She was a brainy wee lass; but like all women she had expensive tastes. She was hard at

work to get the King to come round to her way of thinking. Malcolm and his mates had to fit themselves out with fur and velvet as well as the best of jewellery, looking like a right bunch of royal poofters. The royal tables were set out with gold and silver dishes. Margaret was also a religious nut and she set about bringing religion into Scotland.

As for Malcolm he did what his wife told him and kept his gob shut. Mindful that he had to keep his promise to William. After 7 years of parading about like the biggest poof in the Kingdom, he started to drift back to his old ways.

In 1079, for no apparent reason, other than being bored out of his brains, or there being nothing on the telly, he set about invading England again. His invasion of Northumberland was brutal to say the least. Needless to say, this hacked off William a little and he said 'fuck you pal' and invaded Scotland again. Then to get his point over to Malcolm, William set about building a 'New-Castle' on the Tyne.

This did the trick for the next 12 years. Then in 1091, a dude who went by the name Wullie Rufus took over from William. Whilst he was on holiday in Normandy, Malky got up to his old tricks and invaded England again.

This time, Maggie's brother came back from Flanders to lend a hand and try his luck at getting his throne back. Malcolm however was more interested in what was in it for him i.e. how much he could plunder, than helping his brother-in-law getting his throne back. The Normans quickly retaliated. Malcolm as usual said 'oops sorry it'll no happen again.' Malcolm of course was telling fibs and in 1093 he got stuck into England again. Only this time he slipped up slightly and got himself killed.

Margaret was heartbroken that her sweet little hubby was no more. So she thought; to heck with this and died 4 days later. The difference between Malcolm and Margaret was indeed wide. He was a brutal selfish git whose only real interest was booty. She was a saintly wifie only interested in helping the poor, and as a reward for being a goody-two-shoes; Maggie was made a Saint.

The Norman influence over the years took hold on Scotland. Although they had a strong hold in Scotland they never ever took control. For the next 30 years after Malcolm was no more, Scotland was in turmoil as a number of incompetent Kings followed. The first was Donald (where's yer troosers) Ban, a dude who had a charming last name, which meant 'killer.' He came to the throne a craggy old geezer aged about 60.

Donny had different ideas from his brother, so he started to pursue his own policies. Needless to say; Mr Rufus wasn't overly chuffed with this. It was time for Wullie to play his 'joker'. He sent Duncan, Malcolm's son by his first marriage, who he'd been holding as a hostage to Scotland, to dethrone his uncle (oooh sounds a bit painful). Duncan managed to do this without any real problem. He then crowned himself King and almost immediately did a stupid thing and got himself murdered! So Donald got his jobbie back. He didn't hold on to it long; as in 1097 an Anglo Norman army kicked his arse out again. This time he was replaced by Duncan's half brother, a dude with the wonderful name of Edgar (sounds like a bloody horse to me). Edgar was chuffed right down to his little bits with the Norman's help. Over the years more Norman dudes settled in Scotland.

Edgar also had dealings with a dude who went by the daft name of Magnus Barelegs, this geezer held the jobbie as King of Norway. Edgar being a strong kind of chappie handed over the Hebrides and Kintyre to Mr Barelegs. In truth this was no big deal because the Vikings had held these lands for years anyway.

The only real loss was the Isle of Iona. This had long been the place where we planted our Kings. Thus; craggy old Donald Ban was the last in a long line of Scottish Kings to be planted there. Edgar hit the big snooze button in 1107 and was succeeded by his brother; Alexander I. Alexander was only to rule part of his Kingdom. He was boss man between the Forth and the Spey, thus leaving Argyll, Ross and Moray to their own devices to get on with it themselves. He even left responsibility for the lands south of the Forth to his kid brother Davy. Zanders took himself a wife with the dodgy name of Sibylla (that's the poxiest name I've ever heard of). Sibylla had contacts; her brother just happened to be Henry I of England so, just to keep it in the family Henry repaid the favour by marrying Alexander's sister; the sexily named Maud.

All this of course led to closer ties with England, which of course meant even more Norman influence. In 1124 Alexander snuffed it so therefore he was no longer capable of doing the jobbie.

He was succeeded by the 9th son of his Mummy and Daddy, who also just happened to be his brother Davy (also known as 'Dave the Rave' to his mates). David came to the throne pretty well clued up. He already had a fair bit of experience as the landlord and boss over most of southern Scotland, he was to prove a powerful King. Raised in England were he was taught in the Norman fashion, he grew up with many Norman mates. As well as having the top jobbie in Scotland, he also had a fair bit of clout over the wall. He was Prince of Cumbria. His other half just happened to be a Norman heiress, thus making him Earl of Northampton and Huntington.

One of the first things he did on his return to Scotland, was to start to dish out large estates to his Norman buddies. Davy liked the way the Normans did business, so he introduced features of Norman society and government. Big changes were being made, no fannying about for Davy boy. The Norman way was a feudal one. The land was to be managed by the people, who of course were responsible to the King.

There were one or two obligations; royal revenues had to be strictly administered with accounts inspected. Just to make sure everything was done to the crown's way of thinking, royal officials enforced justice. If you were found cooking the books you could expect a swift kick in the soft and wobblies. The crown officials weren't trusted either and they were checked on from time to time. When it came to defence, the King was still the boss. Poor folk were only too happy to get slaughtered for him. All castles were under his direct control. Castles were the main way of maintaining feudal authority, therefore a mark of power. If you owned a castle you were one of the big boys and the bigger the castle, the bigger the boy! The castles of the day were dark and filthy with running water... running off the walls that is! They were built out of wood with outside staircases. Most were built on top of lumps of ground that were artificially raised and surrounded by water. Filled stagnant ditches (something like your modern day council house!).

It is fair to say that old Davy was the first King to bring in the rule of law, even appointing Sheriffs (they all had the same name; John Wayne!).

Davy was a very religious dude, after all his Mummy was a saint. He set about building many fine Abbeys. One of his grandest was the Abbey of the 'Holy-Rood' in Edinburgh. It is said that he had a jolly good reason for building this one. He was out hunting on the Sabbath, so he obliviously wasn't religious enough to let the Sabbath get in the way of a good day's killing! He was riding through the woods and was stupid enough to get separated from his men. Suddenly a huge white stag appeared, this white stag was no a happy white stag and charged right at Davy. He was knocked from his horse and knew he was in deep shit. The stag turned around and was about to charge at him again when suddenly out of nowhere a silver cloud appeared, out of the cloud came a hand, which held the 'Holyrood' (a piece of Christ's cross). Davy said, 'well hit me with a stuffed kangaroo, is this my lucky day or what.' He took the 'Holyrood' and held it before the stag. The stag, not fancying its chances, vanished. Davy was so chuffed with this, he built or at least he got others to build an Abbey on the very spot it all happened. The story is indeed based on some fact, however the stag was killed by one of the King's men. The piece of the 'Holyrood' was kept in the Abbey until the English nicked it on one of their many raids.

David's reign was, in the main, not a bad one. There were one or two hiccups, one was when Henry I snuffed it. The English King's laddie wasn't too clever at the old swimming game. He was drowned in the English Channel and this meant that the English throne was claimed by his daughter Matilda (also known as 'I'll Give Her a Waltz Alright' to her mates). But she had the slight problem of her cousin Stephen who was the offspring of William the Conqueror's lassie Adele. This put Davy in the thick of it, he was in an awkward position. Henry I had been hitched to his sister sexy Maude, meaning the heir to the English throne was his niece. To add to the problem Stephen had also got hitched to one of Dave's nieces whose name was also Maude.

So what side should he should he support? He gave the matter careful thought and decided 'fuck it' so he invaded on the side of Matilda. No mucking about; his army quickly captured the castles of Alnwick and Newcastle. Meanwhile back at the ranch Davy's son was doing a deal with Stephen on his daddy's say so. Davy being a clever dude had a foot in both camps. Davy wanted a wee thing for himself out of the deal and that wee thing was called Northumbria. Hence in 1138, he put together a large army for a punch up on Cowton Moor. This was to become known as the Battle of the Standard and the Scots came second. So Davy got his own way and Northumbria became Scottish. In 1153 Davy had enough of prancing about playing King so he kicked the bucket. The throne should have gone to Davy's laddie Henry, but the silly bugger had snuffed it so couldn't do the jobbie. The job as King therefore went to Davy's grandson Malcolm IV (also known as 'the Malky-Bar Kid' to his mates). Malcolm came to the throne at the mature age of 11 years.

In 1154, Henry II had become King of England and having a little bit of power behind him, he demanded back Northumbria. This was held by William, Malcolm's wee brother and he wasn't overly chuffed about England getting their sweaty paws on what he considered to be his land.

He was to hold a grudge for many years over this. As for the young King, he wasn't all that impressed with being top notch and keeled over after just 11 years.

In 1165, wee brother William took the jobbie as King. William the Lion (also known as 'A Roaring Good Dude' to his mates), still had a bee in his bonnet about losing Northumbria. His golden moment came in 1174 when England was in turmoil. Henry II was up to his neck in shit over the murder of the dude called Thomas a Becket, a thing Thomas a Becket wasn't too happy about himself. Henry's kids were giving him a hard time. Wullie decided it was time for a little bit of arse kicking so he put together a squad and marched off to Northumbria. Wullie was really in the mood for a good punch up. It was a rather foggy morning and through the mist he noticed troops coming out of the fog. Thinking they were his own reinforcements, the clown shouted, 'over here lads, have some bacon 'n eggs.' He most likely felt just a trifle foolish when he realised he'd just invited the English army in for breakfast.

If you're going to fuck up, do it in style. Wullie at this stage knew he was having a bad day. He was captured, slapped over the puss and tied to a horse, then for good measure they took him to France. Once there he was forced to accept the Treaty of Falaise or he would get another kicking. This basically meant Scotland was ruled by England.

Wullie got out of the nick after a few months but the humiliation was to go on for another 14 years. Wullie was to get his independence back in 1189 from the new English King; a dude who went by the name Richard Lionheart, but only if some dosh was to change hands. He had to cough up to Richard 10,000 marks (£6666 or one heck of a lot of Euros). To raise the cash Wullie brought out a new form of taxation, making him as popular as a heat wave at a snowman's picnic.

Nevertheless Wullie never gave up his claim to what he was determined was his. In 1209 he fucked up again and nearly lost Scotland once more. In 1214 he decided not to bother any more and died.

Wullie was succeeded by his son Alexander II (also known as 'Pany-Zany' to his mates). Alex was a 'chip of the old block' and wanted Northumbria back. Having one or two brain cells he was no daft pudding, so he made a deal with England giving him some extra land. This of course avoided another fight over Northumbria.

Because Alex was a cunning wee dude he became known as the 'Red Fox' by King Johnny of England. Being no muppet Alex was quick off the mark to side with any English barons who weren't getting on overly well with Johnny boy.

Alex enjoyed a good outing so he invaded England five times in just two years. His mates in England being two-faced gits soon deserted him and he had to make peace (most likely jam) with England. In 1249 Alex did the usual thing and snuffed it, the throne went to his young son.

Alexander III (also known as 'Cliff-Hanger' to his mates). Zanders became King at the grand old age of seven. Being a King at such a young age was all very well, but a King needs a queen. At the very old age of ten, Zanders took a wife. He got hitched to a bird called Maggie, her old man was King Henry III of England. She was a mature lass aged seven. Over the next few years Scotland was mostly a peaceful place. In 1272 Edward I (also known as 'Turdhead' to his mates) came to the throne of England. Zanders and his misses got an invite to the coronation do. Not being people to miss out on a free meal they packed their bags and went. Of course there's no such thing as a free meal! Edward wanted and expected Zanders to pay homage to him. Zanders had no problem in paying homage for his English lands.

One of Eddie's English Bishops tried to pull the wool over Zanders eyes and con him into paying homage to Scotland. He took a deep breath and politely replied 'To pay homage for my Kingdom of Scotland, no one has right except God alone.' Having said, 'go and sit on something very sharp and rotate at a great speed' the matter rested for the time being.

Zanders was a lively type of dude and nearly always on the piss making sure there was a nice steady flow of wine in the royal court. In 1275 his wife decided not to be merry anymore and kicked the bucket at the young age of 35. In 1281 his youngest son followed suit and croaked it too. His oldest son thought this was all the rage; so he keeled over in 1284.

Zanders was getting a bit short on the family side of things as he only had his youngest daughter Maggie left. His lassie had got knotted to a dude who went by the name Eric II of Norway, then 1286 she also copped her lot. This meant that Zanders only heir was a wee brat, his granddaughter Margaret the daughter of his daughter Margaret. As for Scotland and Norway they still weren't seeing eye to eye. The Scots wanted the Western Isles back. This of course made a sensible extension to the Kingdom.

Zanders decided to talk business with old crinkle face King Hakon of Norway. Zanders had pulled a fast one. By gibbering on, he had held off his battle with the hairy gits till October thus hoping Scotland's ever trusting weather would lend a hand. The year was 1263 and the punch up was on at Largs.

King Hakon's fleet lay in the Clyde and the gales Zanders was hoping for arrived and blew the hairy men all over the place. The Vikings soon decided 'fuck this for a laugh' so they headed for ground and fought their way ashore. In their rather muddled state of mind they soon got a right kicking on land as well as on the sea.

King Hakon did as all Kings do when up to their necks in it, he bolted. He stopped for a breather at Kirkwall and liked the joint so much he decided to die there. A dude by the name of Magnus (also known as 'I've Started So I'll Finish' to his mates) took over Hakon's jobbie. He made a deal with Zanders and the Hebrides became Scottish.

Back to 1284 Zanders, having lost his heir, knew he was going to have to get his act together sharply. He needed a woman. The following year he was introduced to a bonnie lass who went by the sweet name of Yolande, he thought to himself 'she's a bit of alright eh' Yolande's Daddy held the jobbie of Count of Dreux. Coming from no bad stock and desperate to get his leg over, he got hitched to her.

Six months after they had tied the knot, Zanders was at a council meeting in Edinburgh Castle. After the meeting was over he was feeling a little horny. He had one or two glasses of wine and was now as randy as a dog in heat! As the evening wore on, he became more and more pissed and the more inebriated he became the more he wanted nookie with his beautiful young wife. The problem being she was in Dunfermline Palace in Fife and he on a large lump of rock in the middle of Edinburgh. Thinking with his dick and not his head, he decided he could wait no longer. He mounted his horse and set off for Fife. It was a typical Scottish summer evening; heavy rain and gale force winds.

One old tale tells of when he got to the stormy Firth of Forth he was met by an old crone. She warned him if he crossed the water that night he would never make a return journey. Being a wise old King he listened carefully to what she had to say, then said 'get stuffed ye old hag.'

The tale may or may not be true, but what is true is that he never did make the return journey. He crossed the choppy water and once over the other side he had to make his way up a dark and dangerous path. His horse slipped and Zanders was thrown over the cliff. After banging his head on the rocks several times on the way down he decided to stop breathing. His body was recovered the next morning by his distraught courtiers; it was indeed a sad end for one of Scotland's more noble Kings.

The heir to the throne was Zanders granddaughter, Maggie who was three years old and in Norway. There was however, a slight delay in declaring Maggie queen, as Zanders second wife Yolande; on hearing her hubby had fallen off the edge of a cliff, announced she was up the kite. It was soon discovered she had been telling porky pies. Scotland started to look at wee Mags as 'The Maid of Norway'

All this put Scotland in a desperate position. Maggie's Mum had pooped it just after giving birth and her Daddy was the 16-year-old King of Norway. The heir to the Scottish throne was a mere child; but worse than that; she was not just a child but a female child! To complicate things even more she was hundreds of miles across the North Sea. Scotland was up to its neck in shit. Six guardians took control and it wasn't long before they knew they were in for a rough ride. In vain they tried to control the main families. Most of the big boys all claimed they had a right to the throne. The two main claimants were the Bruce's and the Balliol's, both claimed descent from David I and what's more, both were only too willing to pursue their claims in the manor of the day... with violence.

The Bruce's didn't muck about and seized many royal castles, Scotland was on the brink of civil war. Unlucky for Scotland there was only one geezer with the power and authority to bring order to Scotland. That dude was 'turdhead' himself Edward I of England an evil and ruthless bloke, who can easily be compared to Adolf Hitler. Edward set out his terms in two treaties, which were drawn up at Salisbury at the end of 1289. The following July, it was decided that Maggie was to get the jobbie as queen. Eddie laid down one or two conditions. Maggie was to take the throne under the custody of him; she was also to get hitched to his son. Having laid down these conditions Scotland was to retain her full independence!

Edward of course was fibbing anyway, it wasn't long before his buddies, the clerks started to add little bits to the agreement, which undermined Scottish independence. Indeed Edward was heading towards this when he seized the Isle of Man from Scotland in 1290. Edward had started his long campaign of hatred towards Scotland. As for the young Maggie she was told to get her little arse over here as there was a jobbie waiting for her. Then more bad luck. To Scotland's dismay she was never to set her little mittens on Scottish soil. She proved to be no seafaring kiddie, on the rough passage from Norway she copped her lot with, of all things, seasickness. She died on board the ship surrounded by sweetmeats that were placed there to keep her happy! The wee Maggie was the last in the long House of Dunkeld.

For the next two years Scotland was a Kingdom with no King. It is fortunate that there was respect for the law of the land instilled by the clever dudes from the House of Dunkeld. The claimants to the throne mostly willing to settle their claims at court rather than fisticuffs; sadly the dude who instituted this court was the man who had most to gain, Edward.

It didn't take long before he started to style himself main dude 'Overlord of the Land of Scotland.' The price of his mediation was simple; he demanded that all claimants wishing to get their kneb in and get Maggie's jobbie must do one simple unimportant little thing... Just recognise him as King of England and as their feudal superior!

To get his point over he sent English constables to the main royal castles, and a large army was made ready to give anyone a boot up the arse that got in his way. Having made careful preparations, Edward summoned to court over 100 auditors at Norham. These dudes were to pick the new King of Scotland. This became known as the 'Great Cause.' At the beginning only two chappies came forward to claim the jobbie as King. The dudes were John Balliol and Robert Bruce. They both carried a fair bit of clout. They both had a good claim to the jobbie as they were both descendants of the daughters of David I. The dude Balliol, having a slightly better claim than the dude Bruce, was a descendant of David's oldest lass Margaret. Whereas the dude Bruce was descended from David's second oldest lass Isabel. Bruce, being no onion, had two counter claims against Mr Balliol. The first was that he was the grandson of David, Earl of Huntingdon whereas Mr Balliol was a great-grandson. Mr Bruce's second claim was that Alexander II, before the birth of Alexander

III, had recognised Brucie as his heir. By this stage other dudes were sticking their tuppence worth in for the jobbie. Those who filled in application forms were all chancers. There were a total of 13 claimants, and most of these dudes had about as much chance of becoming King as a hedgehog on the motorway. The reason most of these chancers were trying their luck, was in case it came in useful at a future date.

One example was the Hastings family who were descended from David's third daughter Ad (a name you can always count on). The Hastings therefore thought the Kingdom should be split into three. The kangaroo court sat and listened to all the claims from the very serious to the just plain fucking stupid. One of the most bizarre claims was from wee Mags' Daddy, Eric II. At the end of the day, Edward I was adjudicator and his say would be final. The court made its decision on the 6th November 1292 and eleven days later Edward announced its (his) choice.
The new King of Scotland was to be the 43-year-old dude John Balliol.

King John I gave the jobbie his best shot. By all accounts Mr. Balliol set out to do his best for his Kingdom. He tried to restore good solid rule, letting it be known that anyone who didn't tow the line could expect a good sound trashing. He summoned four Parliaments and established new sheriffdoms in areas that had lost the plot. The jobbie as King was to prove far from an easy one. Things were tricky enough with the disloyalty of some of the geezers who had taken second place in their challenge to be King. Johnny's biggest problem was of course 'turdhead' next door. John boy had been crowned King on St Andrew's Day 1292; three weeks later he had to go off to Newcastle for a wee break. While he was there he had to do something he wasn't overly chuffed about. He had no choice but to pay homage to Edward I. Edward wasted no time in showing his true colours and demanded that any complaints made against King John by his own subjects were to be dealt with in English courts. Johnny was peed off with this idea and told Edward to his face that he was not a happy dude. Edward went ape-shit and immediately threatened John with contempt of court as well as the loss of his three main castles. Edward was turning the screw tighter and tighter. He had imposed humiliating conditions on Johnny to show he was a nothing more than a mere vassal of his. Needless to say at this stage the Scottish nobility were no happy bunnies. The last straw came when Johnny was called to London and ordered to supply men and dosh for England's war with France and the Froggie King Philip IV. Johnny had enough he was taking no more of 'turdheads' crap he immediately made a treaty with the French King in October 1295. If Eddie of England wanted any more he would have to fight for it. This of course is exactly what Edward wanted. The Scottish army liked a good scrap but they were no match for the battle hardened English army. They were strong in cavalry and very skilled in the latest weapon of the day, the deadly longbow. At the end of March, Edward and his chums moved into Berwick, did some sightseeing then slaughtered its inhabitants. The streets were littered with the dead, mostly women and children. Shortly after the massacre of Berwick, John sent a couple of trustworthy guys whose daytime jobbies were Franciscan friars to see Edward. They kicked up hell and delivered a final protest, they told Edward Johnny's thoughts on the matter;

'Caused harm beyond measure to the liberties of ourselves and our Kingdom'

What John boy was saying to Edward was that he could go and boil his heed! Jonno renounced his homage and fealty to Edward, which had been forced on him in the first place. Edward took a benny and full of rage moved into Scotland to try and get his hands on Johnny. On the 27th April, the Earl of Surrey with the help of his Scottish mates; beat up and routed Johnny's army at the battle of Dunbar. Edinburgh Castle fell soon after. At the beginning of July, King John stuck his hands up and surrendered. At Kincardine castle he was made to seal a paper in which he confessed to being a naughty boy by his wronging and folly in allying himself with the enemies of his overlord. Johnny did this even though he just wanted to puke his load. At Montrose, in a humiliating ceremony; he had the insignia of his royalty; his sceptre, crown, sword and ring stripped from him. The family insignia was also ripped from his coat. Edward continued to march north to Elgin on a mission of destruction. Johnny, as a prisoner, was taken firstly to Hereford and then on south where he was given digs at a classy joint called the Tower of London. Edward doing his wheeling and dealing, released many of the Scottish nobles captured at the battle of Dunbar on condition they fought for him in his planned attack on France. In 1299 Johnny was released from doing his porridge and moved to one of his estates in France were he kicked the bucket a blind and forgotten man. King John was to become known in history as 'Tyne Tabard' which means 'empty coat' this is a wicked nickname; it suggests he was a weak man and a weak leader. The truth is he was in the wrong place at the wrong time, with the wrong people behind him and with a ruthless neighbour.

Since Johnny had been removed from the throne, Edward ruled Scotland as King of England. All the Scottish regalia was nicked and sent to London. Edward, being the thieving git he was, demanded the ancient 'Stone of Destiny'. This is the stone that all the ancient Kings of Scotland had been crowned on. The Stone of Destiny is said to have been Jacob's pillow (he must have had one heck of a hard neck). The stone was said to be made of jet black marble, which is interesting because it was bugger all like the stone that Eddie took back to England with him.

There is one tale that may well be fact. What Edward got was not the Stone of Destiny but something entirely different indeed! When Edward demanded that the bishops go and fetch the stone, he didn't have the sense to send someone with them to check they were bringing back the right one. The bishops went to where they did their everyday business, that holiest of places; the shitehouse. They removed one of the larger stones from there and presented it to Edward. He, believing this to be the right stone, took it back to England. For the next seven years, every King and Queen of England was crowned on a toilet seat! When Edward got the stone back to London he had it installed as a trophy of war. One tends to think of this as an odd war trophy; 'one toilet seat.' The real Stone of Destiny was hidden and remains hidden to this day; the place can only be left to guesswork. Under Roslin Chapel just outside Edinburgh is the place it's most likely to be buried.

As for Edward, he started to refer to Scotland as a land rather than a Kingdom. He was

also determined that the British Isles would be one Kingdom ruled by one King... him. Having removed King John, he thought it was only a matter of time before he got his own way and reduced Scotland to a mere province. This bully was in for one almighty shock, the Scots were not about to let him walk all over them.

Many Scots rallied against the evil Edward and paid an horrific price. The most famous was a dude who went by the name of William Wallace (also known as 'Big Willy' to his mates). The easiest way to describe Wallace is 'he was a rather big chap who liked hitting people, especially the English and he was jolly good at it.' Wallace was one of the first to suffer under the savage laws of England. He was almost unheard of before 1297. He is not on the 'Ragman's Roll', a document which Edward had drawn up compelling two thousand Scottish nobles and landholders to pay homage and recognise him as top geezer. Even though he wasn't listed, there was no doubt he came from a family with some dosh behind them. It is not entirely clear why Mr. Wallace took up arms against the English. What is known is that Wullie got into a punch-up with some English blokes at a market at Lanark, his hometown. He was helped to escape by a bird who may well have been his wife. She was captured by the soldiers who, being decent humane people, immediately slit her throat. Her death had been ordered by a chappie called William Hazelrigg who held the jobbie as Sheriff of Lanark. Wullie Wallace was a giant of a man well over 6' (thanks to the film Braveheart, everyone now thinks he was an Australian dwarf). He was mighty pissed off with this brutal murder. The dude Hazelrigg was 'going to get it'. Wallace revenged the murder by kicking the shit out of the Sheriff of Lanark and doing him in. Wullie was 27 years old when he started his campaign to rid Scotland of the English. He was classed as an outlaw, at least in the eyes of the English anyway. Wullie took to Selkirk Forest where he got a group of mates together and built up a band of followers.

The Earl of Surrey and the dude Hugh Cressingham, two of Edward's best mates, were all too aware of the threat posed by Mr Wallace and another Scot, Wullie's mate Andrew de Moray. He was from a small placed called Avoch (pronounced 'Och') in the Highlands. De Moray had been on a short 'family away weekend' to Dunbar, he was silly enough to get himself captured, most likely while building sandcastles. Andy and his old man also called Andy were given digs at a prison in Chester. Not liking the grub much, he escaped. He made his way back to bonnie Scotland to raise an army against Edward. Moray's dudes soon rallied under him, as did the dudes of Inverness. A guy called Alexander Pilche led the Invernessians. Mr Wallace's army was getting stronger and stronger; he was now a force to be reckoned with.

Moray was having great fun; he was kicking butt and was now the new proud owner of some castles, their owners no longer requiring them as they were now dead. He was the boss of all the English held castles in the north. Wallace by this time had kicked out all the English backsides from Perthshire and Fife. The old git Earl of Surrey, the so-called Viceroy of Scotland, was crapping himself. It was becoming very clear what he was up against. He made his way to Stirling, there was going to be one hell of a punch-up.

Someone must have sent a text message to Wallace and Moray, for as soon as they got the news that 'coffin-dodger' Surrey was on his way they joined forces.They made their way to the woods of Stirling, to do a little bird watching and kick English butt. Wullie and Andy were no mugs they knew what they were up against. They were going to have to do some bloody fast thinking. They knew they were up against one of the most powerful armies in the world.They had to pick their ground well, they also had the small task of hiding hundreds of their men. The men were told to keep their gubs shut, there wasn't even to be a fart heard out of them. They were hidden in the grounds of the woods at Abbey Craig.

If things got buggered up the men could still do a runner to the nearby Ochil Hills. Below them was a small wooden bridge. This lump of wood was the English army's only means of getting over the river.

Cocky as ever Sir Hugh de Cressingham let it be known he wouldn't need any more troops, he had more than enough to deal with a bunch of Scottish wasters. The English being fully aware that the Scots had about as much chance as a goldfish in a cattery, offered them a truceThey sent out a couple of donkeys who held daytime jobbie's as Dominican Friars. They were told to go and have a chinwag with Wallace and de Moray. They passed on the message that if the Scots admitted that they didn't have a hope in hell's chance of winning, all they had to do was stick their hands up and say 'ok you win'. If they did this they would not get their soft wobbly bits kicked. Having listened to what the Friars had to say, they told them they would rather become Jehovah Witnesses than give themselves up to the English!

'Tell your commander that we are not here to talk peace, but to do battle and liberate our country', - were the exact words. The Friars were sent packing with their tails between their legs. The English then sent out some boys called scouts to find the Scots army, being unable to notice several hundred very large guys with big pointed sticks. They returned and told Mr Cressingham; no panic the Scots had done a runner. Cressingham however smelled a rat and decided to carry on anyway. On the morning of September 11th the English had their bacon n' eggs and started to make a move. Then they realised something was missing, namely their boss the Earl who was still in the land of noddy, snoring his ugly mug off. So they had to go back and wake him up!

Hugh de Cressingham was no a happy bunny, having been held back. With the Earl now back in the land of the living, the attack was ordered.

Two by two the cavalry led by Cressingham made their way over the bridge. Wallace
and de Moray were cool dudes and in no hurry to kick Mr Cressingham up the hole. They waited 3 hours till half the English army was over the bridge.It was now time to raise the Scottish dudes, heavily out-numbered with very few proper weapons and in the mood for some serious head-butting. The attack took the English by total surprise. The English army found themselves cut off. A large army of Scots with mean tempers stood before them, with a small band of men happily cutting the timbers off the bridge behind them. There was a strong smell of the pongy stuff in the air, as the English army filled their knickers. The English found their horses were bogged down too, so the rest of their army was unable to get over the bridge to help their buddies. Cressingham soon found out what this was all about, he got the point. The Scots spearmen put a sharp end to him. Being chuffed with their prize, the Scots had him flayed.Bits of his skin were sent all over Scotland as a sign of liberation. It's even said that Wallace had a sword belt made out of the skin, which he wore with great pride.

The English were not so cocky now. The Battle of Stirling Bridge resulted in a massacre for them. It is to this day one of Scotland's greatest victories. The Earl of Surrey, because of his extra beauty sleep had not crossed the bridge. He decided the best course of action now was to get on his horse and get the fuck out of there. He bolted away faster than a rabbit with a rocket up its arse. This dude shit himself so much that he galloped his horse straight to the Scottish border. When he arrived his horse was so knackered it dropped dead on the spot.

This battle proved that the humble foot soldier; with a chip on his shoulder was a deadly force to be reckoned with. Andy de Moray however er was silly enough to get himself wounded, he didn't like being wounded so he snuffed it a few weeks after the battle.With de Moray's death; Wullie was now top dog. The Scottish nobles, albeit grudgingly, acknowledged him as number one dude. At this stage Wullie could have grabbed power but chose not to. Being a loyal dude; he governed in the name of King Johnny. In November Wullie and the boys went on a busman's holiday to Berwick where they went mental, totally sacking the town with no quarter given. On his return to Scotland, Wallace was hit over the head with a sword and called 'Sir'. Whoever knighted Wallace is not known, but there is a good chance it was the Earl of Carrick, the future King of Scotland. Wullie was also given the jobbie 'Guardian of Scotland.' His main job was now to prepare for the expected English invasion of vengeance. Edward I of England was now as angry as a bear with a sore head who had misplaced the aspirin. Wallace set about training his army which was mostly made up of common dudes who liked throwing big pointed sticks at other people. In the summer of 1298 the unwelcome visitors came back. Wallace got some of his mates to dig a bloody big hole and stick pointed objects all round it, this was his defensive position at Falkirk, hoping that Edward's army would come here for a punch up. Eddie was going bananas, the Scottish army hadn't come out to play. He was about to rethink his campaign when a Scottish spy grassed the Scots position to him. To Falkirk the English marched, the Earl of Surrey, who had regained some of his 'bottle' after the doing at Stirling Bridge, led his group of English dudes. Edward and Surrey led a powerful force that included hundreds of archers and nearly 3000 cavalry. As usual, the cheating English had twice as many men as the Scots.

The punch up of Falkirk was to prove a right bloody scrap, many a geezer getting a good hard kicking. The Scots fought well against a strong enemy. The spearmen, grouped in their defensive formation, fought bravely until their defences were broken. With their defences down, they soon got their heads kicked in and were slaughtered. The Scots cavalry, mostly nobles and two faced, were still not 100% behind Wallace and quietly buggered off. It was a sad end to a battle where the first English cavalry charges failed to get through the solid wall of Scottish spears. The English archers being no too bad at their jobbies decimated the Scottish ranks. This allowed the heavy cavalry to crash through the gaps made by the arrows. The Scots, despite being heavily out-numbered put on a good show, smashing many a face in and came within a whisker of winning.

The English being chuffed with the result boasted, 'bodies covering the ground as thickly as snow in winter'.

Wallace escaped the battle, pissed off and disheartened but, with his life still intact, he was a tough dude. It would take more than this to break him; he resigned his jobbie as 'Guardian of Scotland.' No one knows for sure what happen next. What we do know is that Wullie needed a wee break so he went off on holiday to Europe. He went to France and Germany then to Rome were he argued his point for the case of Scottish freedom. In vain he tried to get help. Eventually, Wallace came back to Scotland to continue the fight against the English.

Eddie was as nutty as ever and pursued Wallace with the vengeance of a madman. He offered large amounts of dosh to anyone that captured Wallace, he also threaten death to anyone found hiding him. In 1305 Scotland having more than its fair share of traitors Wallace was betrayed. The creep who betrayed him was the dude Sir John Menteith, (also known as scum-face' to his mates) who held the jobbie as Sheriff of

Dumbarton. Here enters one of the most shocking atrocities England ever committed. Wullie was taken; tied and bound with a crown of thorns placed on his head; for the long agonizing journey to London. There, he was put on trial in a kangaroo court. The charges were read out against him. He kept his mouth shut while the English charged him with all the things they themselves were guilty of. The murder of women and children, Wallace still kept his gob shut.

He could hold his silence no longer when he was charged with treason. At this point he blew a fuse.

Treason, how can I be done for treason, in a country that is not mine. I have never betrayed Edward, for I have never taken an oath of allegiance to him',

…Which of course was a very good point, but nevertheless, he was found guilty. Wallace was sentenced to death; his murder was horrific to say the least. He was taken from the court, tied to the back of a cart with his head hanging over, so that when the cart was pulled along, his head banged off the cobbles on the road. This alone would have killed a much weaker man but he was strong enough to take the suffering. He was taken to his place of execution; on the road there he had to pass the spectators. The crowd having been told what a monster he was; threw stones and covered him with every kind of filth imaginable. Once there, he was half hanged stretched until his life had all but left his body. Then he was cut down, his private parts were cut off, and thrown into a fire before his very eyes. He was then disembowelled; his intestines were slowly ripped from his body and burned.

Wallace was now dead and his head was cut off and placed on a pole on London Bridge. The four quarters of his body were dispatched and put on public display at the towns of Newcastle, Berwick, Perth and Stirling.

At this stage, we go from one of Scotland's greatest heroes to another, King Robert I (also known as 'Spiderman' to his mates). Robbie Bruce was born on 11th July 1274 at Turnberry Castle. He was the eighth of his name since the Norman Conquest. Robbie had served Edward several times, but for reasons known only to himself, he grew 'much fucked off' with the English King. At the age of 18 Robbie's old man kicked the bucket and left him the jobbie as Earl of Carrick. Robbie got himself hitched to a lass who called herself Isabel of Mar. Not being very clever at the living game, she snuffed it young. Before she left this planet she had a wee lassie that was called Marjorie, (they mustn't had any butter in those days).

Robbie and his old man had sworn fealty to Edward I indeed his old man stayed loyal to 'turdhead' until the day he popped his socks in 1304. Robbie was indeed confused and torn between loyalty for his country or for his feudal superior Edward of England. Bruce changed his mind no fewer than five times (he should have been a woman). In1297 he sided with Wallace and boldly declared

'no man holds his flesh and blood in hatred, and I am no exception. I must join my own people and the nation in whom I was born'.

Great stuff, this really showed a guy with balls to do as he thinks. Bruce had made up his mind and was sticking to it. A few months later Bruce was back with the English!

In 1302 when Edward offered a truce, Robbie rejoined him thinking it was a plot to restore Balliol by French and Papal sources. It was also about this time the second Mrs. Bruce came along. She was a lass who called herself Elizabeth de Burgh (I know her brother Chris). Robbie was no poor dude in fact he was loaded, his old man had left him a fair bit of dosh. In fact Brucie was one of the richest geezers in all of England. Despite this, he began once again to know where his loyalties lay. The first signs of this were in 1304. Robbie made the 'Bond of Cambuskenneth' with Bishop Lamberton of St Andrews. He was the dude who held the jobbie as head of the Scottish church. Dude Bruce knew he was the guy to lead the Scottish people and being no turnip, he knew if he was going to make a claim to the throne he would need the Kirk in his pocket (he must have had bloody big pockets).

With Wallace's murder Robbie saw himself as the obvious choice for the vacant jobbie as King. He set out to achieve this; in February 1306 he set up a meeting with another geezer who had set his yaks on the Scottish throne. This dude was John Comyn of Bachenoch. He was the nephew of John Balliol. John boy was also known as 'Red John Comyn'. Robbie and Johnny had not quite seen eye to eye in the past and trusted each other as far as they could throw each other! The meeting was fixed in a place of trust and safety, the Grey-friars Kirk at Dumfries.

The meeting was called, no doubt to make plans against Edward I. They met in the church for a wee friendly chat, what they talked about is unknown, maybe the weather, or the price of a good sword. What is known is that Mr Comyn upset Mr Bruce a little bit. Robbie being a reasonable sort of chappie drew his knife and stuck it right into Mr Comyn. Then having decided business was concluded for the day, he left the Kirk. He left 'Red John' very red indeed, covered in blood and dying in the Kirk. So a few of Robbie's closest mates entered the Kirk to make sure Mr Comyn had got the point, to make double sure they all jibbed him several times, until he said 'oh to heck with this for a laugh' and keeled over.

By the standards of the day one noble chappie killing another noble chappie was nothing unusual. Except Robbie had boo-boo'd a little because he had slain Red John in a church. This was a big no-no and nothing less than sacrilege and this meant that in one small fit of temper, he had done two things; firstly he had got himself excommunicated by the church, secondly he had really pissed off the very powerful Comyn family, who had many friends in high places (they knew all the window cleaners).

Robbie now had to watch his step as he was in a very tricky and position. All seemed lost, but Brucie said, 'Fuck it, I'm going ahead.' On Palm Sunday 27th March 1306 having nothing else better to do that day, he raised the Royal Standard and crowned himself King of Scots. Despite his earlier cock-up, Robbie must have had the backing of the majority of the Scottish people, if not all would have been in vain. His coronation is one of the strangest ever recorded in Scotland. It was a basic ceremony, endorsed by a bird called Countess Isabel. This lass was kind enough to give Robbie the traditional blessing of the MacDuffs. He also had the backing of his four wee brothers and of his very apt nephew the dude Thomas Randolph. As well as this, he also had; the Bishops of Glasgow, St Andrew's and Moray on his side with some very powerful nobles. King Robert had a hard time ahead, but one thing in his favour was, that the tosspot Edward of England was getting old. Edward, as soon as he heard the news of what Robbie had been up to, went bonkers and, with a savage bust of fury, he and his army make a beeline for Scotland. Like an astronaut with a wasp in his helmet, Edward was hopping mad and devastation was widespread. Towns were burned to the ground, all who came in his path were put to the sword. Bruce and his buddies had a wee punch up with the English at Methven, things didn't go to plan and they came a poor second. At this stage Robbie did what all brave Kings do...he did a runner. Robbie was now a hunted refugee. He decided to use some big monkeys and launch a guerrilla campaign; this was to be nothing less than military genius. While Robbie was playing hide and seek, he hid in a number of places. One of these was the Isle of Rathlin. It is here that one of the best known stories of Bruceoriginates. It is the story of Bruce sitting on his arse in a cave feeling about as pissed off and beaten as a dwarf in a dwarf-throwing competition.

He began to watch a spider build its web, (I didn't know spiders had computers), no matter how many times the web fell to bits the spider would try and try again until it succeeded.

This is said to have given Robbie new heart for his guerrilla warfare.The story of the spider is a good one, but it's also a load of old cobwebs, dreamt up by Sir Walter Scott in his 'Tales of a Grandfather.'

During the months in which Bruce was keeping his head low, Edward's vengeance was unbelievable; the guy was a complete fruitcake. Bruce's three brothers were captured and duly executed. Robbie's wife and young daughter as well as his two sisters were taken prisoner. Twenty of his best mates were strung up.

Despite all this Robbie kept his campaign going and then, at last some success. At the beginning of 1307 the tide started to turn and in the spring, Brucie and his chums destroyed a large force of Yorkshire-men at Glentrool. In May an even greater victory, this time they kicked the shit out of a major English army at Loudoun Hill.Things were indeed starting to look up for Robbie. Then one of the best days Scotland has ever had, July 7th and Edward I did Scotland a big favour, he kicked the bucket! The prat was on his way back to Scotland when he snuffed it, his last request a simple one. His dead body was to be carried to Scotland, to be present while the Scots were destroyed!

The self-proclaimed 'Hammer of the Scots' was the most resolute enemy Scotland had ever known. During his rein he burned and wasted the whole of Southern Scotland. His hatred of the Scots was only equalled by their hatred of him. He also united Highlander and Lowlander against him. His successor was his sweet little son Edward II (also known as 'Fairy' to his mates), who was about as useful as an ashtray on a motorbike. There is no doubt that Eddie II being a much weaker man than his pa-pa helped the Scots. Despite this Bruce had done a remarkable jobbie, it must be seen as one of the most extraordinary feats of military and practical skill in the entire history of Britain. In other words he did an alright job.

Edward II, having problems with his men friends in his domestic life, gave up his campaign in Scotland. He went back to England leaving his English garrisons in Scotland to get on with it themselves. This made him about as popular as toothache. Robbie was cock-a-hoop and began to push towards the north. In the winter of 1308 he got into a fight with his old buddies the Comyns, who still thought Bruce was a piece of shit. Then in the summer, he led a campaign against their mates the MacDougall's. For this Robbie became the proud new owner of their stronghold Dunstaffnage. By now he was boss man and in control of most of Scotland north of the Forth and Clyde. 1309 was proving a good year for him, he successfully held a Parliament in Fife and at the same time, the King of France, albeit secretly, acknowledge Robbie as King. In 1310 he got the backing of the Church of Scotland, despite the small fact of his excommunication. Brucie was going from strength to strength. In 1311 he took some of his chums on a wee holiday to northern England. There they had a great time burning Durham and Hartlepool to the ground, it was payback time.

Over the next three years the English had their butts kicked out of Perth, Dundee,Dumfries, Roxburgh and Edinburgh. Only Stirling was now in the hands of the invader.Edward II only now realised he was in big trouble and would have to do something bloody quick. He marched north with a large and fully equipped bunch of dudes, his army was to relieve Stirling. It was there that he found Robbie waiting for him and ready to give him a good hard kicking. The battle of 'Bannockburn' was in the making.

This punch up took place on the 23rd and 24th June 1314. Bruce's army was outnumbered three to one; Bruce being a cool cucumber had chosen his ground well. He placed his troops on the high ground tricking the English to advance over the waterlogged stretches of land through which the 'Bannock-burn' runs.

The English Knights heavily mailed (must have got all their post just before the battle!)found their horses collapsing under them; this was caused by spiked potholes which had been placed there by Robbie's men. He had also chosen his ground in such a way that England's deadliest weapon could not be deployed. The English archers. They had been used many times in the past with very deadly effect, but here they were useless. Robbie being a clever bunny knew full well that the archers needed the freedom of movement; he chose the ground denying them this. The English army consisted of some 5000 Welsh foot soldiers, some long-bowmen, 16,000 northern Englishmen and 3000 cavalry, they fancied their chances. The battle started with a small punch up between two old mates. One was none other than King Robbie and other was an English dude who went by the name Henry de Bohun. Robbie was out checking his troops; he was on a small pony with very little armour on. He was out in the open when he was spotted by de Bohun. Bohun who was on a horse16 hands high and in full armour, he placed his lance forward and charged at the Scottish King. The Scottish army looked on horrified, knowing that if their King was done in, all was over. De Bohun going at great speed headed straight towards Bruce. When he reached him, Robbie jumped from his pony withdrawing his small battle-axe from his belt. Managing to avoid de Bohun's lance, Bruce hit de Bohun a right sore one over the back of the nut. He hit the back of de Bohun's head with such strength that the axe went right through the head armour and also right through his nut. The head simply parted in two. It can be safe to assume that this was a little bit of a morale booster for the Scots; as the Scottish army went on to win one of the greatest victories ever on Scottish soil. England's best had been mowed to pieces. Mr. Bruce had one com-plaint however; he had broken his good battle-axe!

Edward moved south faster than a dose of Epsom-salts going through the system, firstly to Dunbar and then on to England. The victory of Bannockburn didn't end the wars with England, but sure did put Scotland in a much stronger position. There were many small raids, sieges and truces. Then in 1318 Berwick, the last English stronghold, fell. At long last the Scots were totally free of the English. Being pains in the butt the English dragged the war on for another 14 years only this time Brucie was playing them at their own game. He started invading England and doing unto them what they had done to Scotland. Robbie even moved the war to Ireland; there the people took heart from what had happen in Scotland.

The Irish even gave the jobbie of King to Bruce's brother Edward, but most likely wished he hadn't bothered as he got himself killed upholding it. Edward II kept on trying to take Scotland and kept on failing miser-ably. In 1322 he attempted yet another invasion. This time he got his frag-ile arse kicked all the way back to Yorkshire (I'll bet he felt a real pud-ding), losing all his personal baggage in the process. Eddie tried everything he could think of to damage Mr. Bruce. Pope Clement V the dude who excommunicated Brucie in 1310 popped it, so Eddie wrote a wee note to Pope John XXII to reconfirm the excommunication. In doing this he set a cat amongst the pigeons, the nobles and the clergy were totally pissed off with his stupidity.

They all had a get-together at Arbroath in April 1320; where they decided to send the Pope a wee note of their own, explaining the situation in Scotland. This was to become known as the 'Declaration of 'Arbroath'.

FOR AS LONG AS BUT A HUNDRED OF US REMAIN ALIVE, NEVER WILL WE ON ANY CONDITIONS BE BROUGHT UNDER ENGLISH RULE. IT IS IN TRUTH NOT FOR GLORY, NOR FOR RICHES, NOR HONOURS THAT WE ARE FIGHTING, BUT FOR FREEDOM - FOR THAT ALONE. WHICH NO HONEST MAN GIVES UP BUT LIFE ITSELF.'

The Pope had a good read of this letter and thought to himself 'these Scots are no that bad a lot.' He still hadn't made his mind up about Robbie, but after a long think he agreed to annul Robert's excommunication. This of course was a kick in the nuts to Eddie who had once more failed. Having had a long line of failures as well as, er being a little more than friendly with his male friends, he was deposed by his wife. He was then tied face down, then a red-hot poker was rammed right up his anus. He lived and died... a pain in the arse.

There were of course further attempts by the English at invading Scotland, but these didn't amount to much and usually resulted in them getting their own arses kicked. The English were beginning to realise that taking Scotland was going to be no pushover, so they began to get bored with war. In 1328 a new attempt was made for peace, the English sent an envoy to Norham and a 'Treaty of Peace' was signed between Scotland and England. We were now the best of buddies. This treaty recognised Scotland as an independent Kingdom and Robbie as King of that Kingdom. To prove the two Kingdoms were now buddy's Robbie's laddie David needed a wife, so he got hitched to Edward III's wee sister Joan (also known as 'bloody moan' to her mates). Davy was chuffed to his little bits with her; he was four years old and his wife, an old woman of seven. The marriage took place on the 16th July 1328. The very next year Robbie fell to pieces. He had contracted leprosy.

Bruce had turned around the events in Scotland by 100%, he had turned a damn near subjugated country into a fully independent one. Credit not only goes to Bruce but also to the people of Scotland who, under strong leadership, fought and died for a free Scotland. In the space of twenty years Robbie had moved from being a loyal servant of an English King to a great Scottish hero who united the Scottish people and gave them a new sense of pride.

The story of Bruce does not end with his death. While Robbie was still alive he had one main ambition, other than kicking English arses. He always wanted to go on a crusade like his Granddaddy had done to the Holy Land (always be careful if you go there, in case you fall in one of the holes and break an ankle). Robbie's bestest mate the 'Good Jimmy Douglas' decided his mate should go on a crusade even if he was deed. So he cut Bruce's heart from his body, put it in a silver casket and hung it round his neck. He then set off on holiday to the Holy land.

This was to prove not one of his better ideas as the silly sausage got ambushed by the Moors in Spain and after getting a kicking... copped it. Just before he was killed he ripped the casket from his neck threw it a cracking distance. A few months after this a dude who went by the name of James Lockhart, found the locket with the heart still in it. He being a damn good fellow brought; it and the body of the 'Good Douglas' back to Scotland.

The heart of King Robert I was buried at Melrose while his body was buried at Dunfermline.

With Bruce no more, the throne went to his wee laddie David II (also known as 'the wee brat' to his mates). He came to the throne a married man at the mature age of five!

The dude Thomas Randolph, a strong chappie and a sound leader, took the jobbie as Regent. Six days before the last piece of Bruce had dropped off and the news of his death could have reached Avignon, Pope John XXII authorised Robert's coronation and unction by the church, this was one thing that was always denied the Scottish Kings.

So therefore it was Davy and not his old man who was the first Scottish King to be inaugurated with full ecclesiastical ritual. Dave was crowned and anointed on the 24th November 1331. The service was conducted by the Bishop of St Andrews. The ceremony took place at Scone and Davy was so tiny they had to make a small Sceptre for him to hold. Davy was not in for an easy reign, the English, with Robbie gone, decided to get up to their old tricks again, now that we weren't buddies any more. They started to renew their attacks on Scotland. The King and Queen were sent somewhere safe to play.

They were packed off to France with some of their toys. They stayed at a joint called Chateau Gaillard, they were looked after by a dude called Philip VI who held the daytime jobbie as King of France.

The kiddies didn't have to flee Scotland just because of the English, there was another reason. The other reason went by the name of Edward Balliol, son of King Johnny Balliol.

Edward III in England was trying to establish himself after the muck-up his mummy Isabella and her sidekick Roger Mortimer had made. One of his first acts was to denounce the treaty of 1328. Which this charming chappie considered as a shameful concession of English rights!

He therefore gave his support to Mr. Balliol. Tommy Randolph snuffed it, therefore giving up the jobbie as Regent. He was succeeded by a dude who went by the name of Donald, Earl of Mar. Mr. Balliol with the help of some of his chums, who were no happy bunnies at losing their lands during the wars. They still hadn't received a bolt in compensation so decided to have a little fisticuffs. They launched their own invasion. They won a punch up at Duppin near Perth, giving Donald a kicking. Being chuffed with themselves, they had Mr. Balliol crowned King. No being very clever at the King game, Balliol was barely able to hold power and what slender power he had, soon collapsed.

The following year the English came back, this time led by their big-shot Edward. He stuck his nose in at Halidon Hill and then took Berwick. Then he had the cheek to restore Balliol as a vassal King. Just a few years after the Bruce, Scotland's independence was once more at risk.

With all of this going on, it was considered one of the better ideas to have Davy and his misuses moved to Froggyland. The Scots were chuffed with the co-operation given by the French.

The Scots led by Tommy Randolph's laddie, nephew of Robert Stewart gave the English a good Fight. Six years of guerrilla warfare followed.

The English launched massive expeditions but found they were getting nowhere fast. Having all but cleared the English from Scotland, the 17-year-old King Davy was brought back from France to his Kingdom in 1341. Some breathing space was given to Scotland by the fact that England was now fully engaged in a little punch up with France. A short wee scrap that was to become known as the 'Hundred Years War.'

During this breathing space Stirling and Edinburgh were recaptured. Then in 1346 the French came second at the punch up of Crecy. The King of France therefore asked his mate Davy for a wee favour. Could he be kind enough and cause a little diversion. Davy was right up for this, unfortunately Davy was no way near the soldier his old man was. He set out with an army to England. This was to prove a rather silly thing to do. At Neville's Cross (why was Neville so cross?) near Durham, his army had its butt kicked right sore, and was routed.

Many Scottish nobles were killed including the dude Johnny Randolph, many were also captured. But the biggest fish to be captured was King David himself. He was to remain prisoner of the English for the next 11 years. In one way this pleased him as it removed him from the cares and burdens of running Scotland.

With Davy his prisoner, Edward once again moved back into Scotland with his puppet Mr Balliol. Once more Scotland was thrown into guerrilla warfare only this time the Scots had the upper hand. The English had no hold beyond the Border. Rab Stewart once again took the jobbie as Regent. In 1355 the Froggie's who were having a hard time of it, once again asked Scotland nicely for a wee hand. This time the Scots made a better job of it and the English got a good hiding. Berwick was taken and the English came a very poor second at the punch up of Nesbit Muir.

Edward III came back from France and not in the best of moods, he invaded Lothian.He and his chums destroyed what they could, but were soon forced to withdraw their army. His army had no grub to nosh and were not happy bunnies at all. Edward was beginning to realise his raids on Scotland were never going to achieve anything other than plunder and destruction. He had now come to terms with the fact that the question was no longer Scotland's freedom, but on what terms Davy would be released.

With the 'Treaty of Berwick' 1357 the terms were made for Davy to be set free from English captivity.

The price was one hell of a lot of cash, the incredible sum of 100,000 merks and because of the large amount of dosh involved, the Scots were given 'easy terms' arrangements.

This meant they could pay in ten easy instalments, this however was only allowed if the Scots also provided 23 of their main dudes as hostages. Scotland at least for the time being was at peace. Edward III was kept at bay with the odd payments of cash; he was also tricked into believing that he; or one of his family would get the throne of Scotland if Davy should snuff it without an heir. David II never once did homage to Edward. Davy's reign was a long one of 42 years... but he only ruled for 18 of them.

These were hard times with near constant wars and ravages of the Black Death which even led to outbreaks of cannibalism. Despite the fact that some dudes were eating other dudes, the economy recovered. This let Davy build up the best financial position Scotland had ever been in.

Davy ruled as boss with strict authority, he wasn't afraid to boot arse if you stepped out of line, even the geezer Rab Stewart was thrown into prison and had to do some porridge.

The reason he was kicked into jail, he had slagged off the King's wife who held the jobbie as Queen. Edinburgh had become the regular centre of government. Davy having got hitched twice, proved to be a jaffa, (as in orange with no seeds) so he had no kids, he died from lack of breath in 1371.

He was to be succeeded by his nephew Robert Stewart. Robert Bruce's daughter Marjory had married a noble chappie of Breton descent; Walter the Hereditary High Steward of Scotland. This marriage is important as this is where the royal name of Stuart comes from. The name Stewart has been corrupted by Scots tongue to Stuart.

Robert II (also known as 'Rab the Humper' to his mates) came to the throne at the age of 55. Rab was the first Stewart King and had to prove himself. He had done a no bad jobbie as Regent but being King was a different kettle of fish. As things turned out Rab was about as much use as a square wheel.

He aimed to give Scotland peace and prosperity; luckily for him the

English at this time were busy with their wee scrap with the Frogs. This kept their minds off Scotland. Money however was beginning to get a little tight; Scotland was being hard pushed by the continuing payments to England. The nobles of the main families began to fall out with each other. Rab should have stuck his oar in to sort things out, but instead he just flung a deafie.

With the barons being allowed to get their way and kick whosever's heads in they liked. Law and order in Scotland became a joke; Scotland was now a lawless state. Dudes were free to kill, rob or do whatever they wanted and their crimes would go unpunished, jolly good fun to be had by all. Robert II was all but a cripple when he came to the throne, a poor King and Scotland became a dodgy place to live. During his life Rab was a prolific womaniser, he was twice hitched, had 13 kids to his two wife's plus a few more to ladies he was not married to. It's fair to say, this guy could shag for Scotland.

After 13 years of weak government Rab admitted that, when it came to doing the jobbie as King, he was crap.

He handed over control to his laddie John, Earl of Carrick. Four years later Johnny boy got on the wrong side of a horse's hoof and copped an unfortunate one.

Johnny was just about as good as his old man was at doing the jobbie, about zero.

The jobbie for the time being went to another one of Rab's kids, the over keen Earl of Fife. As for the people of Scotland they decided there was no government. Things were not looking good, and then on 19th April 1390 Robert II became totally useless and kicked the bucket.

The throne went to John, Earl of Carrick. The first thing Johnny did was to decide he wasn't going to be called Johnny, as he considered it an unlucky name. Hence Johnny became known as (Julie) King Robert III (also known as 'Rab the Loony' to his mates).

Rab came to the throne a cheery sort of dude who was also a cripple and a manic-depressive.

He was totally unfit to rule before he was crowned and therefore was totally unfit to rule after he was crowned. After his coronation his brother the Earl of Fife, whose name was also Robert; except he had the name first, was given the jobbie as Governor of the Realm. Thus King Robert III allowed his Kingdom be run for him or to be more precise miss-run for him.

The country got more and more like a rabble. Lawlessness got even more out of control; vassals screwed their superiors for dosh rather than land, forcing an even bigger strain on the King's fast disappearing income. This became known as 'Bastard Feudalism.'

Robert III also had a brother who was a bit of a bad egg; he went by the name of Alexander but was known to his buddies as the 'Wolf of Badenoch.' When Rab came to the throne Alex took the huff and went on a tour of mass destruction with some of his mates who were also rotten eggs. They went down in history as 'Wild wicked Highland men.' Alex and his chums were about as popular as an elephant with severe flatulence. He got too big for his boots and pushed his luck too far when he burned down Elgin Cathedral.

This proved to be one of the most notorious acts of medieval Scotland. Alex tried to "cry wolf", but King Robert and his brother Robert were having none of it and Alex well and truly got his wrist slapped. After a good telling off the 'wolf' crawled into his den and quickly faded from the scene.

King Robert and his brother Robert had teamed up together to kick their brother's arse. Before long they were at loggerheads with each other. So after a few years Robert kicked Robert's rear end and sacked him.

Rab now took the reins himself. The result, the country went more and more to pot, law and order was a total joke. In 1399 someone else had to be found to do the jobbie, therefore the jobbie was handed to Robert's oldest laddie David, Duke of Rothesay.

Dave held the jobbie for a whole three years, even though he was the boss man he still had to work hand in hand with others. One of these was his uncle Robert who no longer went by the title Earl of Fife, but was now going by the name Duke of Albany. Dave worked his backside off and in 1401 he had a few new law reforms brought in.

Dave was having one or two problems with his private life, he had got himself into a little bit of a pickle. He dumped a lassie he had been knocking off, who just happen to be the sister of the Earl of Crawford. Then for good measure he did the same to another bird, but she was the sister of the Earl of March.

Then, deciding he had enough fun, he settled down and got hitched to the Earl of Douglas' sister. Dave soon found out you could pick yer mates but no yer family. His brother-in-law soon sided with Dave's uncle Robert, Duke of Albany.

The pair arrested the young Dave and kicked him into prison in Albany's stronghold Falkland Castle. It was in this castle in 1402 that Dave was no more. There is no proof to who done Dave in, but the finger of suspect points towards Albany.

During Rab's reign there was a widening gap between the Highlands and the Lowlands. The southern part of Scotland was being seen as prosperous and cultured which was in marked contrast to 'what was believed' to be the uncivilised barbarity of the Gaelic-speaking northern regions. In the north the system of the clans was beginning to develop. At this stage the 'Lords of the Isles' the MacDonald's (crap burgers) were very powerful in their own right. They governed themselves in what could be called; their own state.

In 1396 Robert III himself enjoying a good day out, was a spectator at the infamous 'Battle of the Clans.' The Clans Mackintosh and MacKay were not the best of buddies and decided to settle their differences in a gentlemanly manner. They settled on a fight to the death.

On 28th September at Perth, 30 men from each clan lined up and faced each other. The Mackintosh's soon discovered they were a man short. The problem was soon solved by offering a piece of gold to a saddler who was in the crowd of spectators. The saddler jumped at the chance and took the gold.

When Rab signalled the end of the slaughter; 29 MacKay's lay cut to pieces on the field. Their one survivor escaped by swimming at great speed across the River Tay. The Mackintosh's only lost 10 of their men and the saddler lived to spend his gold.

After Dave's mysterious demise in 1402 Rab was all too aware how close his brother Robert was to the throne. Not being the fastest of movers he decided to safeguard his throne for his only surviving kid; Prince James. In 1406 in secret, he had the young Jim placed onboard a merchant ship bound for France and safety. Even this gesture of goodwill went pear-shaped. Robert III who had about as much luck as a fire-eater with hic-cups; had fucked up again.

The ship was captured by pirates who couldn't believe their luck when they found out what the cargo was. Jim was handed over to the English usurper Henry IV. The English King was kind enough to give the young Prince Jim digs in the usual place, the Tower of London.

When news reached 'lucky white heather' King Rab, it was the last straw, he could take no more; and therefore took no more; and was no more within a few days... he snuffed it.

During his lifetime Robert III had said of himself for a future epitaph, 'Here lies the worst of Kings and the most miserable of men' and to boot asked that he be buried in a 'midden' The second part of his statement may well describe how he felt but the first part is not true. He was as weak as a wet fart when it came to doing the jobbie as King but against all the odds, he did what he could.

With Rab deed and his heir held captive in England, Albany was quick to take control and became Regent. He had some opponents but they ceased to cause him any trouble when they all met with very sudden and mysterious deaths. Not surprisingly most decided to work with Albany. He had taken the jobbie as Regent at the coffin-dodging age of 60 odd and was well over 80 when he dodged his coffin no more in 1420.

In Albany's time as Regent, not a lot happened in Southern Scotland. In the North it was a different matter, the jobbie of keeping the place in order was given to a dude called Alexander Stewart, who held the title Earl of Mar. He was the bastard son of the infamous 'Wolf of Badenoch' and, unlike his Daddy, he went from a Highland freebooter to a government agent and even made his mark on the European stage.

During Albany's time, relations with England were mostly peaceful. It was during this time that he managed to get his laddie back, he had been their prisoner for a number of years. Negotiations went on and on for the release of King Jim. They never succeeded, which suited Albany just fine. In all fairness it was English policy to keep King Jim in England and even more so during Henry V's reign, he wanted to keep the Scots at bay so he could go to France and do some Froggie bashing!

King James I (also known as 'Codmouth' to his mates); Jim didn't get the best of starts or finishes for that matter, he was held prisoner in England for 18 years (that's the worst torture imaginable, being in England for 18 years)! Jim under tight English guard was kept prisoner. The English however were kind enough to give wee Jim a good sound education. He was able to make good use of his natural qualities (I'll bet he did!) he was a fit young chappie with a very sharp mind. Henry IV kept a close eye on Jim and let him share in the ways of the Lancastrian court. There's no doubt Jim was fair chuffed with the goings on around him. Being a smart cookie he developed a real love for learning and literature.

While Jim was living the life of Riley, the Scots folks back home weren't too chuffed that he had not been returned. Jim was being held in a foreign country against his will, being no onion he used his yaks and lugs to find out and learn all he could about the English ways of things.

Then in 1423 he copped his peepers on something very interesting... he saw, he wanted and he got. What he saw was a young bird that went by the name Lady Joan Beaufort she was one of Henry's cousins. She was a tidy bit of stuff and Jim fancied her rotten. He was head over heels in love, she was a wee cracker and a good catch.

The happy couple got hitched in 1424. She nagged him to put quill to paper and thus James I became not only King but also a poet to boot.

Jim just before his marriage, agreed to the 'Treaty of London', this would allow him to come back home to bonnie Scotland. He could come home at long last, but only if the Scots paid the cost of his digs and grub over the last 18 years as well as the cost of his travel home.

After a quick calculation the English released King Jim for the nominal sum of 60,000 merks, about £40,000 quid. In April 1424 Jim and his other half crossed the border. He was crowned at Scone on the 2nd May.

Things thus far had gone well enough for Jim but his troubles were just beginning. For those who had ruled Scotland in their King's absence, his return only meant one thing for them...disaster.

Jim was in his Kingdom and was going to rule with an iron fist. Right from the start he was taking no shit and set out to bring law and order to his country. The first to feel the end of the royal boot was the house of Albany. They had done alright for themselves while Jim was in England. Jim's action was swift and ruthless he made sure several members received hair cuts... from the neck up! Their lands were annexed to the crown, which pleased Jim as this returned power and dosh to him.

Jim was showing he was the 'head' dude by removing anyone's head he

considered in the way. Anyone who was out of order who didn't ю
heads lost their lands.

Jim was a callous git he was a hard man in what was an unruly countɪy
he was bringing Scotland back into order. By doing so he was making
himself one almighty unpopular chappie.

In 1428 he went to Inverness for a wee bit of Nessie spotting on Loch
Ness. While in Invershneckie he ordered 50 of the main Highland chiefs,
which included big shots like Alexander, Lord of the Isles to meet for a
chinwag.

The Highland Landers were no thick gits but Jim had tricked them into
thinking that he was coming around to their way of thinking. They certainly had no idea what he had up his sleeve. As soon as they all arrived
in Inverness Jim greeted them by having them all arrested and thrown
into the local nick.

The ones he was not overly happy with, he had executed by his
favourite method, beheading.

After their heads were removed, he had them stuck on poles round
Inverness Castle, most likely quite decorative.

The poles were all different heights, the more important you were, the
higher your head was placed.

Who says size doesn't matter!

All Jim's acts in the North of Scotland only achieved one thing; He was
really pissing the Highlanders off and distancing Highland culture from
the crown.

Jim could not or would not trust any of his feudal inferiors. He changed
the rules and brought in many new measures to bring Scotland into order.
Such as the regulation of dress and the fish protection of salmon. He
made sure that the learning of archery was increased as he had seen
English bowmen in action and knew only too well how deadly they were.
Other acts Jim brought in included the organising of fire fighting and
brothel-sitting (my kind of job). Another act which should perhaps be
brought back today was the banning of football (the way the Scottish
team play this could be a good thing!). Learning was also increased and
Scotland's first university was founded at St Andrews in 1412.

Jim had his up and downs with the Papacy but this didn't mean he was-
n't a man of the church. In fact he was very much a man of the church and
would quite happily order the burning of heretics.

One of the main reasons Jim was able to get on with his way of doing
things was the fact that England was far too busy trying to hang on to their
Froggie possessions.

In 1428 Jim renewed the 'Auld Alliance' with his French buddies. The
'Treaty of Chinon' made available 6000 Scots soldiers to fight for the
French King.

In 1436 the Anglo-Scottish truce was no more. In the punch ups that
followed Jim failed to recapture Roxburgh from the English, this was the
start of his rapid downfall. He needed more time to get all his enemies

he did not have. In February 1437 Jim was at home having cuppa with his wife, Queen Joan. They were at the
ary at Perth, they had not a Scooby that some of his very
ects were about to pay them a wee visit.

was led by a chappie who went by the name of Sir Rab
had dealings with Jim in the past and had come a poor second. Jim had few mates even in his own house, servants unlocked the
doors and were even kind enough to lay planks of wood across the moat
for the would be assassins to cross.

The pissed off conspirators burst in on the defenceless Jim, it is said
that one of the Queens ladies, a lass who went by the name of Katherine
Douglas tried to stop the baddie's getting to the King by thrusting her
arm through the bars of a door in the royal apartment to give him time to
do a runner.

Katherine received for her troubles; an arm that was broken in several
places. As for Jim this gave him but a brief respite. Knowing the nasty
bugger's were coming to do him in, quick thinking was called for. So in a
gentlemanly manner, he calmly started to rip up the floorboards to get to
an underground drain and escape. Except for one slight problem he overlooked in his haste. Just a couple of days before, he had the drain blocked
up because he kept losing his tennis balls down it. He was to lose more
than his balls this time!

The no very happy Mr Graham and his buddies quickly cornered Jim.
He tried to do some fast-talking explaining he was King and 'they all better fuck off or else'. They were having none of it. To get their point over,
Jim was stabbed 16 times. Beginning to get the point, or points, the King
did the time honoured thing and died.

Queen Joan got stuck into the attackers herself but she got a good slap
across the mush for her troubles. She was now one very very pissed off
Queen. She ordered that all the conspirators be arrested, and she would
personally draw up their executions. This bird was no happy about her
hubby's murder at all.

The two main bad eggs were Sir Rab Graham and the dude who wanted the crown for himself Robert II's last surviving laddie; Walter, Earl of
Atholl. Queen Joan wasn't holding back; her methods of execution were
barbaric to say the least, even in those hard times. Mr Graham was taken
to his place of execution. He was given the honour of being slaughtered
first, as it was believed he was the one who actually had done the King in.

His young infant son was placed before his eyes then the child had his
throat slit from ear to ear. Then Sir Rab's hand was nailed to the wheel
of a cart so he could be dragged along the road, at this stage he did a
rather unsporting thing…he died.

By this time Queen Joan was really hacked off and she wanted her
revenge. This meant that the Earl of Atholl was to take the full brunt of
the punishment. His execution lasted three days. On the first day every
joint in his body was dislocated when he was thrown from a crane. Then
he was tied to a horse's mane and dragged along the ground in excruciat-

ing pain. On the second day, an iron crown was made for him, after all he did want to be crowned King. Before the crown, which bore the words 'King of Traitors' was placed on his head, it was put into a red-hot fire, then the burning hot crown was placed onto his nut. He was then once more tied to a horse's mane and dragged through the streets only this time he was burned with red hot pokers as he was pulled along. On the third day, and amazingly he was still alive, his balls were cut off and thrown into a fire before his very eyes. Then his stomach was ripped open and his intestines were slowly pulled out and thrown into the fire, then his liver and his heart were burned. Being most likely dead by this time his head was cut off and stuck on a pole. His body was quartered with parts being put on public display in Edinburgh, Stirling, Perth and Aberdeen.

It is fair to say that the mild mannered English lady was more than just a little annoyed with them. At least another 40 of their mates met with a similar fate. James I was known as the poet King,

> 'I am King I am,
> I am King I am,
> and I've got a,
> Ding a ling,
> cause I am a
> King I am'

He was the most forceful King Scotland had known in over a hundred years. He was an unusual chappie because he had that very rare quality, he had no problem in being ruthless and a hard nut, yet at the same time, he was a very talented poet. When Jim came to the throne, Scotland needed a strong King, he came to the throne a strong man and he ended his life in a place of strong smells, a stinking pit.

In the 14th and early 15th century Scotland wasn't exactly the 'in' place to be, in fact it was fucking awful, times were a little hard to say the least. The way of life hadn't moved forward much in the last few hundred years. Most folk all had one thing in common they were all skint and most lived in the countryside for the lovely fresh air. They would be lord of their mansions in their dwellings.

The average size of a house in those far off romantic days was 20ft long and about 15ft wide. The luxury pad would consist of two rooms, one for the folks to live in and the other for the livestock to live in. For the privilege of living in one of these mod con apartments they had to pay rent to the lord of the land. He being a kind and understanding landlord would charge extra rent when there was a good harvest.

The crops in those days were mostly oats and barley. The best dish of the day was to take one sheep; remove all the good eatable parts and throw them away, then take all the parts that taste like shit, cook them in the sheep's stomach and, bingo you have one lovely dish... haggis!

To add to the joys of medieval life in 1349 along came a little thing called the plague the 'Black Death.' This was a nasty little bug, which was spread by fleas from black rats.

'Ring a ring of roses'
A pocket full of posies
Atishoo Atishoo
We all fall down'

The population of Scotland during this time was about one million. In those days, if folks were not happy about something they wouldn't put up with it, so they mostly dropped dead. It's not known how many copped their lot with the plague, but what is known is that the population dropped sharply by at least by a third. That's a heck of a lot of dead dudes. It took Scotland nearly a hundred years to get over the ravages of the 'Black Death.'

James II (also known as 'pizza-face' to his mates) came to the throne a cool dude aged six. He was to become known as 'James of the Fiery Face' because he had a huge birthmark slapped right across his ugly coupon. He grew up feeling paranoid that people were staring at his marked face. His paranoia was indeed based on the fact people were inclined to gawk at his ugly mug. It was this that helped develop wee Jimmy into the man he became, a cunning two-faced toe-rag with a temper to match. Although Jimmy was only six when he came to the throne, he did not take over as jobbie of King until he was 18 years old in 1449.

In the same year, he got himself hitched to lass who went by the name Mary of Gueldres. Her uncle was a dude called Philip the Good of Burgundy, he was a good dude. She herself was said to be a no-bad bit of stuff. Jimmy had come to power and like his Daddy, he was ready to rule with an iron fist and take no shit. His upbringing hadn't been all that smooth; in 1440 he was at the infamous 'Black Dinner' when wee Jimmy's pa-pa was done in. It was the usual squabble for power amongst the big shots. The Earl of Douglas got the jobbie as Regent and he was one heck of a powerful chappie. This geezer had a fair bit of clout in the property market. In addition to the Froggy lordships of Touraine and Longueville, Mr Douglas owned more estates in bonnie Scotland than any other git!

Things were beginning to look like he was going to take complete control. Just as things were looking good for him, he fucked it up by dropping dead.

He left two young laddies who would one day cop all his wealth and power. Others with their fingers in the pie were the dudes; Sir Willie Crichton, who held the jobbie of Governor of Edinburgh Castle. It was Mr Crichton who also held the jobbie as the wee King's guardian. Being a cunning git, he came up with a cunning plan. He jumped at the chance to destroy the power of the Douglas household. He enlisted the help of other bad eggs such as Sir Alexander Livingstone who held the jobbie as

Governor

of Stirling Castle and Jimbo Kennedy who held the jobbie of Bishop of St Andrews.

The late earl's sons were to be at the butt end of Crichton's plans. The oldest lad was Wullie, he had the jobbie as the new Earl of Douglas. His wee brother and sidekick was called Davie.

Crichton's plans to get rid of the two young kids suited their uncle James 'the gross', with the boys disposed of... this creep stood to inherit all. The plan was put into action. The two young kiddies were invited to a slap up meal with the 10-year-old King at Edinburgh Castle. On the 24th November, Earl Wullie and his wee brother peas n' gravy sat down to the nosh up with the King in the Great Hall of Edinburgh Castle.

King Jimmy and his young cousins got stuck into their grub. As they were stuffing their faces, they had a little bit of a chinwag. Most likely about who had the best toys. As they were gibbering away, a 'black bulls head' was brought in and placed before the two little boys. The kids shit themselves as this was the symbol of impending death. Jimmy pleaded for his young chum's lives but to no avail. His two young cousins were removed from the table and taken outside. They were then both beheaded, the young Jimmy witnessed this. He kept his head, which was more than his cousins did. James II then did what all brave Kings do; he sat in the corner and sobbed his heart out. The 'Black Dinner' was to affect Jimmy for the rest of his life.

When Jimmy took the reigns of power, he took a leaf from his old man's book. Any of the nobles he didn't trust, he had their estates removed and given to the crown. Jimmy however still had the problem of the big bad Douglas dudes. James 'The Gross' and his sidekick, who was also his successor. Willie had done a no bad jobbie at rebuilding their family's power. Jimmy tried every trick in the book to destroy the powers of the Douglas mob. He even sent the 8th earl of Douglas Willie on a wee holiday to Rome in1450.

Jimmy's sneaky wee plan was to snatch all the Earl's lands while he was in the land of pasta. This cunning little manoeuvre failed, so Jimmy had to resort to plan B.

He summoned Willie to Stirling Castle in February 1452. He was given a safe pass to the castle with the usual promise that he wouldn't have his head kicked in and the usual promise of safe conduct.

At the meeting, over some nosh, King Jimmy asked Willie to stop winding him up and maybe they could become buddies. So could he be a nice chappie and do things the King's way? Earl Willie listened to what Jimmy was saying, and then he told the King to get stuffed and go and boil his head! King Jimmy being a reasonable kind of chappie drew his knife and stuck it right into the Earl, right sore. At this stage all the Kings' mates joined in the fun... there's nothing to beat a good stabbing; fun to be had by all, except maybe the Earl of Douglas.

The Earl, having been jibbed several times, did the usual thing and died. Jimmy had not planned the murder but he certainly lost no sleep over it, he carried on pursuing the Douglass's till their power was broken in 1455.

After Jimmy had finished with the Douglas's he got on with the jobbie of being King. He travelled round Scotland, and at the same time he kept his eye on the borders to keep the English in check.

He got chatting with Norway over the Western Isles. In 1458 parliament was so tickled pink with Jimmy and all his hard work, that they passed a special vote of thanks. They also gave him a pat on the back for the way he was maintaining law and order.

Jimmy had a hobby, he loved firing his cannons; big guns were a powerful new invention. Jimmy was able to get a good supply through some chums of his wife. He wanted to know all there was to know about these weapons and considered himself a smart-arse on the subject, there wasn't anything Jimmy didn't know about his cannons.

Affairs with England were starting to go downhill fast. Things were going to pot over the wall; the useless government of Henry VI had upset their own folk. All the big shots took sides in the dispute, which for some stupid reason was to become known as the 'War of the Roses.'

In Scotland the Douglass's went on the side of the house of York. King Jimmy gave his full backing to Henry VI and the Lancastrians. It was at this stage that the Yorkists chappies fell from power; James was right on the Douglas' case, booting their arses all the way.

He used his new weapons well, and one by one the castles of the southwest were blown to bits. One of Jimmy's new weapons was called 'Mons-Meg'; it was the nuclear weapon of the day. A giant, built purely for wide-scale destruction.

Mons Meg was a weapon to be feared. Unfortunately it wasn't very practical. It could only fire two cannon balls every hour!

In the summer of 1460 in support of Henry VI, Jimmy laid siege to Roxburgh. Being in a good mood and awaiting the arrival of his wife, who was coming to view the proceedings, Jimmy wanted to show off what he could do with his cannons. He decided to fire off in front of the Queen. However, the special big bangs he arranged in his wife's honour, were not one of his better ideas.

One of the cannons failed to fire. Jimmy decided, being an expert on the matter, to go over and see what the problem was. He stuck his head up the cannon to check it out, unfortunately for Jimmy there was no problem. The cannon was in the process of misfiring, it blew up, taking tiny pieces of the King of Scotland with it. The explosion killed Jimmy outright. King James was truly a man over his subjects!

A few days after the King was blown to tiny pieces, Roxburgh was taken by the Scots. As a mark of respect the great historic stronghold was totally and utterly destroyed. After James of the Fiery Face met a fiery end, his son succeeded him; he also went by the name James.

James III (also known as 'Paramecium-Brain' to his mates) came to the throne at the ripe old age of nine. The first ten years of his reign went smoothly enough. He was lucky enough to have his mummy, Mary of Gueldres to give him a helping hand.

In 1469 Jimkins tied the knot with a bird that went by the name Maggie of Demark. Maggie's old man no being short of a few bob, offered 60,000 florins as a dowry. It was soon found out that he was in fact, very short of a bob or two and was skint. So instead of the dosh he gave Jimkins Orkney and Shetland. This was a good catch for the Scottish crown. Jimkins was chuffed to his royal bits with this as it brought the Stewart Kingdom to its fullest geographical extent.

Maggie must have been some cookie because at one stage she was even considered by the church for Canonisation (I wonder why they wanted to eat her?) Jimkins had one or two problems with some of the powerful families, but soon kicked their arses into gear. One such was MacDonald, the fourth Lord of the Isles. He had got chummy with Eddie IV of England in 1462. He made a pack with him. This pissed Jimkins off mega and indeed was nothing less than treason. Jimkins put him in his place in 1476 and he was forced to give up his earldom of Ross. Jimkins being a laid back kind of dude liked the finer things in life. He was fair taken with good quality jewellery. He personally overlooked the minting of his coinage, making sure it was greatly improved, at least for the time being anyway.

He also had a fine collection of classical manuscripts. He was a guy of the arts. Scotland and England had more or less been at peace since 1464. This suited Jimkins' just grand cause as a man of the arts, he wasn't too much into the rather messy business of killing.

Jimkins wanted the situation to stay the way it was; therefore he was doing his best to cement this with a marriage alliance. His joker was the marriage of his sister, big Mags to Edwards IV's brother-in-law the Earl of Rivers.

There was a slight problem with this plan. Big Mags had been a naughty girl and was having it off with a dude who went by the name Lord Crichton. What's more she was up the stick with a bun in the oven.

Jim was beginning to look a bit of a prat and his rule was going into a state of chaos. Things went from worst to worst and Jimkins trusted almost no one; he started to get paranoid about his two brothers and the respect they were receiving.

No being a happy bunny, Jimbo had The Duke of Albany and the Earl of Mar arrested in 1479. Albany decided sod this for a laugh, so he did a runner.

The Earl of Mar wasn't quick enough off the mark, and knew he was in deep shit. Jimkins had heard some rumours about his brother wee Johno, the Earl of Mar and some witches. Johno was henceforth dispatched. He died in the bath; some say it was a clean death. Others say that he was bled to death and murdered.

In England all the loose scrapping that had been going on, turned into full-scale war. Jimkins brother that did the runner was hailed as King Alexander IV of Scotland. Now this really cheesed Jimkins off to say the least. An English army led by his the brother of the English King started to head north. The threat of an English invasion gave the nobles the balls to speak their minds.

Jimkins lugged in to what they had to say, he wasn't that overly interested in their moans. Despite this he had the cheek to ask for their support to kick English arse. The nobles were having none of it, they were just no happy with the King's favourites. In fact to get their point over they grabbed six of them and hanged them over Lauder Bridge.

Jimkins himself was taken to Edinburgh Castle and was not allowed out to play. The upset of Lauder didn't do him any great harm though and before long he was in control again. Within a year Jimkins had given the English army a doing and one of the leaders who got his nuts kicked was Jimkins brother Albany. One of the main reasons Jimkins managed to gain power and defeat the English was the small fact that his brother Duke of Albany forgot he was going under the name King Alexander IV, and became one of Jimkins closest buddies… most likely because his nuts were aching. The English King's brother Richie was as confused as a lobster having a hot bath! He retired his army back to England, but not before he took Berwick. As for Jimkins good buddy his brother, he decided he wasn't his best mate after all and in 1483 he left Scotland and got it together with the exiled Douglas.

Once again he attacked his brother the King. Jimkins was still no taking any of his shit, so once again Albany failed. Deciding he was getting nowhere fast, Albany went to Froggieland and took up the peaceful past time of watching tournaments. Perhaps not one of his better ideas as within a year he was accidentally killed while watching one. King Jimkins was still a bit slow in the up-take and his subjects were just no happy with him at all. People were pissed off at his unwillingness to uphold the law. Gone were the days of his good coinage, he cared not and was turning out cheap nasty coins. The barons were not a happy lot about the way he was running his court. All this led to one thing in 1488. Rebellion, leaders were the Home family and the Earls of Angus and Argyll, they all had the support of the Bishop of Glasgow.

It is even said that it was the King's own wee laddie Prince James himself who challenged his old man to a square go. Jimkins quickly called his still loyal subjects to arms. Many rose, mostly from the Highlands. There was to be a big punch up at a place called Bannockburn. Therefore it was known as the Battle of Sauchieburn.

The weakly led royal army got a right good kicking and was cut to pieces. One story tells of King James doing a runner from the field, mounted on a grey charger. In his hand, the sword that once belonged to

Robbie Bruce.

His horse stumbled and he was thrown to the ground. He was carried clueless and shaken into a nearby mill. There he was asked who he was and he replied 'I was your King this day at morn' then believing he was about to stuff it, asked for a priest to give him his last rites. The miller's wife ran outside; there she stopped a passing stranger who claimed that he just happen to be a priest! As a man of the cloth he would give the King his last rites, all right. He entered the mill, lent over the King and proceeded to give him his last rites...by drawing a dagger and sticking it right through the King's heart. Jimkins took the hint and promptly gave a loud yell and crocked it. What really happened to King James at the Battle of Sauchieburn is unclear. It may be the case that his death was an accident; the silly bugger might have just fallen off his horse.What is known is that he died with very little, if indeed any chums.

King Jimkins was indeed a complicated chappie and it has been said that his reign was an 'irrelevance to the throne.' It is true he was ill suited for the jobbie as King. However James did reign for 28 years, during which time he had to content with a fair bit of grief. Things like endless lawlessness, economic troubles, his two-faced brother and barons who would go out their way to stir the shit.

Despite this he injected a lot of good things into his time as King. For some strange reason, credit due has not been given to him, he was succeeded by his laddie James.

Folks in 15th Century Scotland could not understand James III, to them a King was the all powerful-one. What they had was a geezer who was useless at riding a horse and hated the idea of violence. In fact the thought of killing made him want to throw-up, he also preferred his own company to that of anyone else.

Life in 15th Century Scotland for the poor was just that, poor. For rich dudes it was just a little better. Those with the dosh would have larger pads to crash out in. Furniture was very basic; in the hall for example there would be a large dining-table. This was removed at night so the servant's could crash out on the floor.

There were no such things as carpets or cupboards. The big shot that was usually a lord would have a big oak chair for him to plant his rear end on. This was placed at the head of the table; everyone else would have get comfy on a bench with no back on it. Grub was served up in wooden dishes or if you were in luck pewter. Things indeed might well have been basic but 'etiquette' was the order of the day. Men always carried their own knifes; forks were just about unheard of. So being told to 'fork-off' in those days was very rare!

When it came to eating, the order of the day was that the food be carried to the mouth with two fingers and thumb only and most certainly not fistfuls.

James IV (also known as 'know-all' to his mates) came to the throne aged 15 and feeling a little sheepish about his part in his Daddy's demise. He did not kill his old man, but the barons had taken advantage of his youth and inexperience. They used this to con him to going on their side.

For the guilt of this, Jim wore an iron chain of penance round his waist for the rest of his life. He was to prove the most impressive King since 'The Bruce.' He had an incredible zest for life and lived it to the full.

He wasn't afraid to show he had balls and was admired for his physical courage. He had buckets of self-confidence and was more than willing to listen to others before he made any decisions.

Even though Jim lived life to the full, he never forgot to worship and would even 'fast' two or three times a week. In fact in those gluttonous days when one would stuff as much grub in one's puss as one possibly could, King Jim was known to eat very moderately. Unlike others who would stuff their gob till they threw up.

Jim was a clever little poodle and could gibber in several foreign lingo's. He was also the best-known King to all his subjects, travelling round the country almost non stop. Jim did have a slight weakness he was a horny git. Being over friendly with the women folk meant he had an awful lot of kids running about calling him Daddy.

He became known as the 'Renaissance King.' Jim's love of the ladies led to one of his most serious affairs. He had been banging a lass who went by the name Margaret Drummond. Jimmy had the hoots for her in a big way. However the ways of the day and a bowl of porridge were to prove her downfall. Jim was head over heels with this bird and it is believed he got hitched to her in secret. As always there was the problem with England.

Henry VII had a brainwave, a way of cementing everlasting peace between Scotland and England. He wanted his wee lass who went by the name Margaret Tudor to get hitched to Jim. This in itself wasn't too bad an idea, as it would give the Scots an interest in the English throne, something that actually bore fruit a hundred years later. There was no way this marriage was going to go ahead while Maggie Drummond was on the scene and giving Jim one.

This problem was solved one morning when the King's wife, mistress or bit on the side or whatever, sat down to breakfast with her two sisters. They decided to start the day with a nice healthy bowl of porridge.

The porridge must have been slightly off as the three of them dropped dead from poisoning. It has never been found out who the bad eggs that killed her were.

Some say King Jim himself had a hand in it. This seems a little unlikely as he showed much grief in the fact that his sweetheart would eat no more porridge.

With Maggie Drummond done in, the path was now clear for the marriage to go ahead. Jim wasn't overly chuffed about it at first but got use to the idea of the marriage of the 'Thistle and the Rose.'

Jimmy rode out to meet his new bride to be, he was a man of 30 and much experienced in the old shagging game. She was a lass of 13 and clueless in the ways of the birds and the bees. King Jim accompanied her on the last part of her journey into Edinburgh. Having a liking for the finer things in life Jim laid on one of the biggest do's Scotland had ever seen. Music, dancing, decoration lots of grub the pageantry was a sight to behold.

He had splashed out a small fortune on clothes for himself and his pages. On the big day itself, King Jim showed who was King and wore a white damask gown, crimson sleeves in his jacket, a cloth of gold doublet, he in fact looked just the bee-knees. As for wee Maggie herself she liked the idea of dressing up as well, her clothes were brought from England. Like any other 13 year old she was a little bit short of clothes, so it only took twenty-four carts to bring her gear to Scotland.

Maggie was a sour-faced grumpy kind of lass, her arrival and marriage in 1502 was the first time Scotland and England hadn't wanted to knock each other's blocks off without a truce since 1328. This was to last less than a decade. Maggie also brought with her to Scotland a dowry of 10,000 English pounds. This no doubt pleased Jim as he was getting a little strapped for cash. Her next jobbie was to provide the King with bairns so he would have an heir to the throne. She soon got down on the job and between 1507-1514, she spat out six kiddies.

However five of them didn't fancy being royal much and stuffed it in their infancy. King Jim took a keen interest in every aspect of Scotland, even the ever-recurrent problem of the Scottish Highlands and their clans. It was during Jim's pa-pa's reign in 1462 that as stated, Johnny, Lord of the Isles made a pact with Edward IV. Jim's old man kicked Johnny's butt for that, but Johnny's out of wedlock laddie Angus Og was a mean git with a temper to match. Angus had got himself hitched to Argyll's lassie. He soon decided his old man was out of order so declared war on the King as well as his Daddy. This split the Highlands in two causing the Macdonald's to fall out with the Macleod's and the Mackenzie's in a big way. At the punch up of 'Bloody Bay' in 1480, Mr. Og having won the scrap, took his Daddy and two of his mates Maclean of Duart and Maclean of Ardgour as his prisoners. Angus was proving what a bad egg he was, a chappie who had a keen liking for applying violence. He kept the Highlands in a state of fear and turmoil. Mr. Og had one soft point, he liked the sweet music of the harp. One day his reign of terror was no more; his harpist gave him ear-to-ear music by slitting his throat.

It didn't take long for the punch up's to break out again. On a cheap day return to Inverness, its castle was seized and then nasty things happened to the lands of the Mackenzie's.

The Highlands were in a state of total unrest. Jim was mega pissed off with Johnny, Lord of the Isles, he was now an old git. Jim stuck one on his hooter and took his lordship from him. Old Johnny moved down south and kicked the bucket a broken man in a Bed 'n' Breakfast for dossers in Dundee in 1498.

King James decided to do something none of his family line had done before. He went on a wee holiday to the wild Highlands of Scotland. Being a brave King he wasn't afraid but took with him an armed guard, just in case.

Jim visited all the nice scenic places, as well as taking a few holiday snaps, he got to know the locals. Jim was helped by the fact that he could speak their lingo. He soon made a few mates and got in with the locals for a wee bit of hunting and the like.

He of course was stretching his luck a little, hoping his visits would make a difference to the way of life in the Highlands. Having tried the nice as pie approach and failing, he changed his mind and said 'well stuff you.' He started to shake his royal fist and charters were revoked, Huntly and Argyll were given jobbies as lieutenants of the Isles with the power to kick arse when the need be. Jim had fucked up; his lieutenants were as popular as a copper hat in a lighting storm.

In 1501 a dude who went by the name of Donald Dubh or Black Donald led an uprising. Donnie was good uprising stock as he was the off-spring of Angus Og. As in all uprisings, fun was to be had by all and in 1503, the Macdonald's and the Maclean's held a house warming party in Inverness and burned the town to the ground.

King Jim was able to show who the boss was when Black Donnie was captured. He was booted into prison at Stirling Castle in 1506. Jim established a number of strong points and held order in the Highlands.

As for the Lowlands, things had never been better, it was the in-place to be. Learning was top notch, the arts were going places, culture was the order of the day. On the whole things were looking pretty good.

Jim started looking overseas for some fun, being no daft cookie, if he wanted to kick butt overseas, one must have a navy. So he set about building one. He didn't want just any old navy he wanted the best, so he set about building a great fleet. Not by himself but with the help of others i.e. boat-builders etc.

Jim's pride and joy was his 'Great Michael' she was said to be the greatest ship of her day. She cost a hell of a lot of dosh about £30,000 Scots pounds. This was a colossal amount. One of the greatest ships ever, but her history didn't amount to much and she ended her days by being flogged to France. They got her for the bargain price of £18,000. The pride of the Scottish navy which was 150ft long weighing 1000 tons with a crew of nearly 300, she ended her days as a rotting hulk in the Froggie port at Dieppe.

Scotland was looking good but Jim's brother-in-law Henry VIII (also known as 'fat git' to his mates) opened his gob and claimed that he owned Scotland; a showdown was just a matter of time.

Henry was a sportsman and his sport was war. In 1513 he invaded France. Jim was putin the near impossible position, which of the ally's he was going to side with? The Queen of Froggieland sent Jim a nice little teaser. It was a turquoise ring with it came a letter asking him to be her champion and take the Scottish army one-foot into England, to divert the English from their war with France. Jim being a sensible kind of chappie blew all caution to the wind. He liked the ring.

Jim decided to take the 'Flower of Scotland' on a wee trip over the border to England. One of the worst disasters Scotland was ever to know was in the making.

The punch up of Flodden, this was to be the mother of all fuck up's, a great dent for Scottish pride. Jim a King who united both Highlander and Lowlander led one of Scotland's greatest armies into England for a cause that was sod all to do with him. A force of 20,000 legged it into Northumberland. They took Norham Castle and a few other strong points. This was before they met the dude who went by the name Tommy Howard, Earl of Surrey. He was old crinkly git who had his laddies with him to kick Scots butt.

They had with them an army slightly smaller than the Scots, but with the best of gear. King Jim had plenty of bottle and was good at the jobbie of being King. When it came to the jobbie of being a general, he was as about much use as a chocolate mantelpiece.

Tommy the Earl of Surrey was fully aware that Jim was no great scrapper. In those days chivalry was everything, so the big punch up was arranged for the 9th September 1513.

King Jim took up the best defensive position on Flodden Edge. He stood his ground and refused to move from his position till the agreed date of the punch up, even when he had the chance of attacking the English while they were split as they moved to cut off his supplies.

The day of the battle came and Jim decided he was to show he was one of the boys and would lead from the front. The two armies were well matched, but the English cannon were to prove better than the Scottish spears.

King Jim knowing what was best, led his buddies down hill in a ragging attack, there was no stopping them. That was until they got to the bottom and ran straight into marshy bog, this put a slippery halt to the Scottish advance.

By this time tempers were high. The order of the day was to meet as many English as possible, face to face, say hello and then run your sword through them. Jim was in at the thick end of the punch up and at one stage came within feet of the Earl of Surrey. He was on his way to say hello to him, when some English decided to say hello to Jim first, they said their pleasantries... then cut Jim to pieces.

The battle of Flodden was lost. Scots and English losses were high, the 'Flower of Scotland' had been given a good solid thrashing. With the King, thousands fell including his own laddie Alexander, others who fell included at least nine earls and thirteen barons.

Jim was a strong King who insisted in most to do things his way and did things his way till the very end. His mutilated body was found the day after the scrap amongst the corpses of his common subjects, whom he had led into a pointless battle.

Half the Scots army lay dead on Flodden field, a blow Scotland was never to fully recover from. The English were sliced to pieces and were unable to follow up their victory by an immediate invasion of Scotland.

The Scots defeat was a shocking event; one of the best Stewart Kings had been lost as well as most of the Scottish nobility and for what? A shitty little turquoise ring. The jobbie of getting Scotland back together was left to Jim's laddie Jimbo.

James V (also known as 'Jim the Miser' to his mates) came to the throne at the grand old age of 17months. In Scotland's favour was the fact that it was nothing new to have a kiddie on the throne. So the Scots just got on with it.

King James IV having an idea that he might one day be on the wrong side of a sword left a will. In it he stated that his wife Maggie was to be his son's guardian.

That was all very well but there was no way she was getting the jobbie as Regent. She was after all the sister of Henry VIII, whose army had just kicked the shit out of the Scots, Henry was also eager to get his paws on Scotland.

Maggie Tudor had always stayed loyal to her brother. She was so upset with the lost of her hubby on Flodden field that the following year she took a new hubby. He was young dude who went by the name Archie Douglas, 6th Earl of Angus.

Her reasons for her new marriage are unclear, perhaps she was just lonely, never the less her jobbie as guardian to the wee King was removed forthwith. The jobbie as Regent was filled by a chappie who went by the name John, Duke ofAlbany, his old man was Alexander brother of James III. Johnny had been brought up in Froggieland were he was born. He had spent a lot of his spare time in the French army and was in full favour of the 'Auld Alliance.' His jobbie as governor of Scotland was confirmed by parliament on 12th July 1515.

Maggie, like it or not, had hand over the kiddie, this she did then buggered off to England with her new hubby.

There she bore him a wee lassie who went by the name Margaret Douglas, who herself had a wee laddie who went by the name Lord Darnley who was to very much feature in Scottish history.

As for Maggie's new hubby Archie, he soon got bored with her and got chummy again with Albany. It was this that led his uncle, the famous poet Gavin Dunbar, to call his nephew 'a young witless fool', there's nothing to beat good old family support.

Albany got on with the jobbie of being Regent, this he did well despite his long holidays in onion-land. In 1517 he negotiated the 'Treaty of Rouen.' In this he made a deal that King Jimbo would get hitched to Francis I of France's daughter.

The treaty itself was ratified by the Scots parliament in 1521, after the wee lass was born. She went by the name Princess Madeleine. Jimbo and Mads got it together and tied the knot in 1537.

Albany was only too happy to offer Scots help with Francis Ist's punch up with the English. At the siege of Wark Castle the Scottish army decided they had a good view and watched their French allies scrap with the English. In 1524 Albany took off to Froggieland, he was never to return.

During Albany's time there was the usual bickering with the powerful families who all wanted to get their sweaty hands on the reigns of power. The Douglas's and the Hamilton's were at constant loggerheads with each other. One incident came to a head in Edinburgh in 1520, this became known as 'Cleanse the Causeway.' Cardinal Beaton (also known as 'whore Master' to his mates) of the Hamilton mob was a powerful and wealthy chappie. Even though he was a man of the cloth, ladies of negotiable virtues were often seen leaving his house in the early hours of the morning.

The house stood at the bottom of Blackfriars Wynd. The Cardinal was about as welcome as a fart in a spacesuit, and the good folks of Edinburgh had it right up to their back teeth with him. They were only more than willing to lend a hand to get shot of him and his mates from the town. Their chance came soon enough.

Gavin Dunbar on hearing there was to be trouble went to the Cardinal's pad to find out if the rumours were true. Beaton answered the door with his full robes on, when Gavin asked if there was any truth in the rumours. Beaton started to beat his chest like a gorilla that just had his bananas nicked and said 'Sir, on my conscience I have heard no such rumours.' As he started to beat his chest there was a loud clattering sound from under his robes. To this Gav replied 'Sir, your conscience clatters', clatters having a double meaning one being that he was telling porkies the other being the clattering sound from under his robes was caused by the heavy iron mail he was wearing underneath. Beaton knew full well there was going to be a fight. A few hours later in Blackfriars Wynd the Douglas's and the Hamilton's came to fisticuffs. The good citizens of 'Auld Reekie' leaned out their windows to watch the fun. They asked passers by if you were a Hamilton or a Douglas, if you said you were a Douglas they would hand you a weapon such as a knife to get a Hamilton. If you said you were a Hamilton they would still give you the knife, but in the back.

The fighting raged on for several hours and at one point Cardinal Beaton knew he was beaten and bolted into the small Blackfriars church at the bottom of Blackfriars Wynd for safety. Unfortunately for him, he was spotted and followed in by two Douglas's, they were about to slit his throat. Gavin Douglas appeared and saved Beaton's life by declaring they could not kill a man of God in the house of God, to which Mr Beaton replied 'thank God.'

Beaton ended his days as an ambassador in France. After the skirmish of the 'Cleanse the Causeway' the streets were littered with dead, the blood was flowing down the causeway like water. The Hamilton's had been cleared from the town.

Maggie Tudor had made her way back to bonnie Scotland in 1517 having promised to behave herself; she regained the guardianship of her son on Albany's flight to France.

King Jimbo was now 12 years old. Maggie had the full support of James Hamilton the first Earl of Arran. Maggie was enjoying her little bit of power, but at a price, her high and mighty brother Henry VIII was sticking his oar in.

He was no happy with her over her divorce, as he being a total hypocrite was fully against the idea of divorce! A bit like the pot calling the kettle black.

Henry had found a new way of carrying out his schemes in Scotland, his sister's ex hubby the Earl of Angus was doing all he could to support English policy. Things were going his way and in 1525 he gained control of young King Jimbo. In the same year it was agreed that custody of the King should be shared by Angus, Arran, Lennox and Argyll, each would have the wee King for three months of the year.

Angus was first to get a shot of the King. When his three months was up, being a fair man he said 'stuff you, yer no getting him he's mine' and refused to hand wee Jimbo over to Arran.

King Jimbo was now a prisoner of his step-Daddy and remained his prisoner till 1528. Angus having his bit of power was making sure he was keeping it. He gave all the top jobbies to members of his family.

His brother a dude who called himself Sir Georgie Douglas got the jobbie as master of the household. His uncle a chappie who went by the name Archie Douglas of Kilspindie got the jobbie of treasurer, other jobbies such as master of the larder went to James Douglas and so forth.

In 1526 Jimbo at the age of 14 was declared old enough to rule, this of course wasn't the case as he was still prisoner of the Douglas's. It was 1528 before Jimbo finally managed to escape the clutches of Angus. He secured himself in Stirling Castle. It was there with his mummy's help he was joined by the Earls of Arran, Argyll, Moray, Bothwell, Eglinton and Montrose all these dudes declared themselves for the King, and stated what a rotten git Angus was.

Angus was far from happy but knew his chips were up. He retreated to the east coast castle of Tantallon. In this stronghold he held out for a few months, but in the end he had to admit that his power was no more. He decided to go on an extended holiday to England, his estates taken from him. The big bad Douglas's were outlawed, all their lands taken from them and any power they had was destroyed.

Jimbo was now free to get on with the jobbie in his on right. He was a level-headed dude; he had received a fairly good education from his tutor

Gavin Dunbar. Jimbo also had a love for music, despite the fact he had a singing voice equivalent to that of a foghorn!

He was a typical Stewart in the fact he had an eye for the women. He set to work ruling his Kingdom, first on the agenda was restoring law and order which had once more slipped into decay. This gave him some respect from his subjects, for the way he set about distributing it fairly.

Jimbo was also known to dress up as a common farmer and wander amongst his people to find out how they lived. The poor had a great liking for this King. The better off with the dosh took a very different point of view. They thought Jimbo was a waste of space a cruel, mean vindictive chappie. The main reason was he was cashing in on their cash. The 'Act of Revocation' gave Jimbo the excuse to demand large amounts of dosh from those who had encroached upon the royal estates.

He was out to make as much as he could, so he took the title Lord of the Isles to the crown. He showed who wore the crown in his Kingdom. He gave the heads of the countries top families new accommodation by throwing them in jail. He was not a chappie to get on the wrong side of. Jimbo also brought in to Scotland the punishment of hanging, drawing and quartering a punishment seen as too barbaric for Scotland up till now.

The first lucky chappie to receive this was the Master of Forbes who was the brother in- law of the hated Earl of Angus. As for the Master of Forbes sister she had the pleasure of being burned on Castle Hill in Edinburgh. Jimbo obliviously enjoyed a good burning as he travelled 16 miles to watch her fry.

He had very little in the way of mates; his only care was to create great wealth. Since 1487 the Pope had been a nice chappie and let the King have a say in the permitting of rich benefices, hence the Scottish church was involved of the every day running of the country. King Jimbo being no mug made full use of this, using the church as a major source of income. Being a clever chappie he called this his 'Great Tax.' To make sure that all was to run smoothly Jimbo appointed five trusting mates to high positions in the church.

These five trusting mates also just happen to be his sons who had been born out of wedlock. He used the clergy more and more, indeed in 1532 it was spotted that there was very few earls present at his councils.

Jimbo the miser had a passion for making dosh and could never get enough. Being as tight as a duck's arse, which is watertight, Jimbo would spend his cash carefully. Important things like a magnificent new shiny crown for his nut. He also had built for himself fantastic new palaces with all the mod cons of the day.

In 1536 he went on a wee trip to France to get himself hitched. When he got there Francis I offered him a lass who went by the name Marie de Vendome. Jimbo clocked her coupon and noticed she had a face like a fish supper, half bashed and full of chips. He had a wee word with his mate Francis explaining how he felt about this bird, most likely telling him he would rather jump in a pot of boiling oil than get it together with her. Jimbo had been offered another bird in the first place. Francis let him have the lass he had been promised. She went by the name Madeleine. Mads was a sickly lass but had a much better coupon than pox-face Marie. Mads was also fair keen on doing the jobbie as Queen.

Love was in the air and they got hitched. Jimbo the miser got himself a wife, but much more importantly he also got a nice wee dowry of 100,000 livres. To boot there was also the odd ship thrown in.

The royal sweethearts made their way back to Scotland. Two weeks after Mads arrived in bonnie Scotland she decided she didn't like the jobbie of being Queen after all and promptly snuffed it.

Jimbo heartbroken by his new wife's demise but took some comfort in the fact that he got to keep all the dosh she brought with her. The hunt was now on for wife number two. The next year Jimbo set his yaks on another French cracker, a lass who went by the name Mary of Guise. He was attracted to her blue eyes and the fact she brought with her a dowry of 150,000 livres. Once more love was in the air and they got hitched.

Jimbo's religious ways were a little odd-ball to say the least. In 1540 he had a go at the very source he was getting most of his wealth from. At the same time he was showing he was indeed a religious chappie. He made a barefoot (you would think with all his dosh he could afforded a decent pair of shoes!) pilgrimage to the shrine of Our Lady of Loretto, a joint just ten miles outside Edinburgh.

King Jimbo was having a successful rein. His policy of full support for the Froggies didn't wear too well with his subjects, they still remembered what helping the onion lovers could lead to. Jimbo had also lost many mates in high places by using all sorts of legal excuses to confiscate their fortunes for the crown; i.e. himself. There was more afoot than just this, he had been no quite right in the head since a hunting accident in 1537. A bang on his nut had left him with bouts of despair. In 1541 his two young kiddies and male heirs to his throne pooped their cots and then popped their clogs. This made him even more depressed.

In 1542 he had a chat with some of his nobles and told them to raise an army to give his pest of an uncle, Henry VIII a kicking. Henry being a pain was once again showing signs of his dislike for the Scots and their ways. Jimbo was told to go and boil his heed, he was met with a stubborn refusal. Many had started to look kindly on the new Protestant religion. For them taking up arms for the Pope was a big no-no, for others, the doing Scotland got at Flodden was still fresh in their minds. What's more they all had one thing in common, they had about as much time for James V as a dose of the Black Death.

Their way of showing the King how pissed off they were with him was not by open rebellion, but by simply telling him to get stuffed and refusing to fight for him. Jimbo still managed to get a few mates together mostly recruited by the clergy. They met the English at Solway Moss, on the

River Esk. Jimbo's army, which now consisted of 10,000, was led by a chappie who went by the name Oliver Sinclair of Pitcairns.

On the 24th November 1542 they came face to face with a bunch of English dudes who numbered about 3000. They were led by a chappie who went by the name Sir Tam Wharton. The odds were very much in the Scots favour.

Ollie was one of King Jimbo's favourites, he was considered by others as a total prick. He led an army that was in no mood for a battle and would have much preferred to be sitting in the boozer. Some started to refuse orders, which was bad enough. Then some started to fall out with each other and decided to kick each others head in. Some of King Jimbo's army just looked at this poor excuse for a fighting force, they shrugged their shoulders turned around and went back home for a pint. Truth was no one was willing to fight, especially the borderers, for a King from whom they had suffered years of persecution.

The excuse for a scrap took place, very few were killed and over 1200 Scots were quite happy to be taken prisoner by the English. Including the King's so-called chum Ollie Sinclair. The punch up of Solway Moss was a disaster, not a great defeat like Flodden but a poor square go that finished with wholesale surrender.

Jimbo was now mega pissed off, a very depressed chappie, he withdrew to Edinburgh then he moved to Linlithgow from there on to Falkland. Were he took to his bed, found it to be so comfy that he popped his clogs in it just two weeks after the battle.

Some say of a broken heart, but most likely he snuffed it due to lack of breath. Jimbo hit the big snooze button at the ripe old age of 30. He is reputed to have said six days before his death, on hearing of the birth of his daughter and heir, Mary 'It came with a lass and it will gang with a lass.'

He was referring to the fact that the Stewart mob started with the lass Majorie Bruce and was now about to end with a lass. If he in fact did say this or not doesn't matter, there were more Stewarts to follow after his daughter.

Queen Mary (also known as 'Frog-head' to her mates) came to the throne at th eridiculous age of six days! She came into her Kingdom unaware what was lying ahead, much trouble for her and a country that was changing fast.

Life in 16th century Scotland was a simple enough affair, the population give or take one or two, was one million. Most dudes still lived in the countryside, well spread out over the Kingdom.

Clusters of people would be found living near a Kirk in their own wee 'farmtouns.' The way of life was to work the land and pay the rent to the landlord. Life was tough and folks had to depend on each other to lend a helping hand. Tenants paid for their digs and would obey the rules laid down by the landlord.

They also looked to the landlord for physical protection from any baddies. The laird of the land would also be a bigshot in the parish Kirk; in fact he was often related to whoever was in charge of the Kirk.

In the Lowlands this worked well enough as they all spoke the same lingo. In the Highlands it was a different ball game altogether. There was the start of a cultural gap between the bossmen, who were bilingual and the tenants who only spoke one language, their own, Gaelic. Landlords and tenants would often employ skilled dudes to do wee jobbies for them. Exciting things like ploughmen who had the enjoyable jobbie of walking up and down a field all day. Pushing a large metal blunt object in such a manner, they were able to see what lay under the mud, usually more mud!

Barnmen known as threshers, what they did with straw is best left untold. Shepherds who were experts in sheep (I'll bet they were!), the jobbie of sheep-shagging, oops sorry sheep-shearing was a tricky and dirty one. So this jobbie was left to the women-folk.

Other skilled workers would include fowlers, limeburners, dykebuilders these chaps were usually stoned. Farmers took great care of their bit of muck, for he and his family depended totally on the land for their survival.

Often the land would be in the same family for generations; once the tenant snuffed it the lease would pass on to his heir. If the farmer grew to become an old git and was too old to work on his piece of muck, he would make out a contract with his kin. They would hand over the farm in return for grub, clothes and a roof over their head.

Life went on as always for the folks who lived off the land, but for the upper class this was a very complicated time in Scottish history.

Mary who is better known as Mary Queen of Scots wasn't even a week old when she was handed the jobbie as Queen. The outlook for Scotland was positively frightening.

Henry VIII, King of England and great-uncle to the wee lass on the throne of Scotland was, for a reason not fully known to this day, the main supporter of Protestantism in Europe.

He had no time for France and the Pope and hated them with a passion and he was determined to be Master of Scotland. He set about achieving this; he came up with the wonderful idea of marrying Queen Mary to his wimp of a son Eddie.

A treaty of marriage was negotiated with Arran who had taken on the jobbie as Regent. Arran was in favour of moving toward England rather than France. The Queen's mummy herself a frog, had other ideas. She had the tiny Queen carried; most likely because she wasn't big enough to walk, to Scone were she was crowned.

To the noble families Henry was an old annoying git doing all he could to get his sweaty paws on Scotland. Henry was politely told 'Go and fuck yerself.' He had but one answer, invade and totally destroy Scotland!

He sent a fleet that landed at Leith. The English army was led by a dude who went by the name Earl of Hertford. On landing at the port of Leith, then on the outskirts of Edinburgh the English made themselves welcome by burning it to the ground.

The English louts then advanced into Edinburgh. The Scottish capital was unprepared for the onslaught. After the battle of Flodden in 1513 an English invasion was feared, there and then. So the people of Edinburgh set about building a huge wall right round the town. This wall was up to 40 feet high and 10 feet wide. It was indeed a brilliant idea, except for one small thing, even though this was now 1544 the wall wasn't finished yet, and they say builders are slow today; in fact the wall wasn't finished till 1560!

On reaching Edinburgh Hertford's mob entered through the gate known as the Netherbow Port, this is roughly halfway up or down. Edinburgh was torched and such was the ferocity of the burning that the English themselves were forced to leave the burning town, because of the density of the smoke.

Thus they were unable to take Edinburgh Castle. As well as Edinburgh the entire Borders were destroyed. The English army returned to England, patting themselves on the back having done a good days work.

Henry once again started opening his gob and demanding that the marriage will go ahead. Once more he was told to 'go and fuck himself'. Again, Hertford was on his way back to Scotland with some of his buddies on a mission to burn or destroy anything they might have missed the first time. It was now September 1545, this time they were kind enough to honour the Scots with a visit of three weeks. They still failed to capture Edinburgh Castle. This period of history became known as the 'Rough Wooing' and you don't get much rougher than that!

Henry VIII the English King was known in England as 'old copper nose', because when he had his coinage debased with copper, the middle would wear away first, revealing his nose as copper. In Scotland he was not known as 'old copper nose' but something else entirely, which is not printable.

Then he did Scotland a huge favour and kicked the bucket. The problem was not over yet. Hertford was now 'Protector' and was now calling himself Duke of Somerset. He had a bee in his bonnet and was determined on what he saw as the 'Protestant Union' of Britain. Once again he tried to use force to get his own way, this time his invasion led to the punch up at Pinkie.

This scrap known as the Battle of Pinkie took place on the 10th September 1547 and once again the Scots got a kicking. The English army numbered about 16,000 including cavalry, artillery and even some naval support.

The Scots army was much less disciplined and very weak in the cavalry department. They were led by a dude who went by the name Sir Bernard Fergusson. Mr Fergusson noticed movement in the English ranks. He thought to himself 'their bottle has crumbled', he was sure they were crapping themselves and about to do a runner.

The Scots gave up their position and Arran shouted 'get into them', the attack was ordered. There was one almighty punch up, men sticking large pointed objects in each other, guys getting hit with big things that went bang and blew them to pieces.

The Scots lost more than 15,000 men, English fatalities numbered less than a 1000. Amazingly Somerset failed to exploit his great military triumph. He did not advance on Edinburgh, this time he most likely realised that Edinburgh Castle was one of the strongest forts in all Europe.

Arran, taking the hint that he was up to his neck in doggy-poo, had Queen Mary hidden in the Highlands. Somerset had kicked Scottish arses well and sore, he was now sure it was only a matter of time before the Scots bowed to his way of thinking. He must have been a fair bit upset when he realised that Arran wasn't going to come round to his way of thinking. Within two weeks the large English army rose from its digs at Leith and started to move home.

On his trip home, Somerset established a series of forts in the south. He was confident the Scots would never be able to overcome these English strongholds. The English garrisons in these forts introduced themselves to the locals, then did the usual thing and killed them. Dundee was left burned to the ground.

Fife didn't do much better and the borders just about turned into shires of England!

Edinburgh was fast becoming the in place to be and was soon crowded with refugees. Queen Mary was taken to the boating pond and put on a ship bound for France. She went for her wee holiday in August 1548, a much needed wee break that lasted for 13 years! She was just a wee lass when she left but when she came back as a big lass, it was to a Scotland where much had changed.

The Scots had struck up a deal with Henry II of Froggieland, they agreed Mary could get hitched to Henry's laddie the future Francis II. In return for letting Mary get off with his son, Henry was to send an army to Scotland.

Once the bunch of Frogs arrived Mary would be on her way. This was shattering news for Somerset, it was the end of his dream of uniting Scotland and England. Everything the English themselves wanted was in fact given to the French. The strong Frog army arrived in June 1548, the English holding on to their strong parts, but not for much longer, they were starting to lose them one by one.

Mr. Somerset had however built some pretty tough forts and getting into them was no easy matter. The French spent the summer of their vacation trying to take the fort at Haddington. In fact there were many up's and down's. The French being their usual nippy selves were beginning to get on their host's nerves, it was only a matter of time before someone got a good sound kicking.

There was an anti-French riot in Edinburgh, this came about after a

French loudmouth picked a fight with a locksmith. The Governor of Edinburgh Castle was walking by when he saw the commotion. He was a dude with much respect by the name of Stenhouse. He told the Froggie to behave himself and go home. The Froggie being the rude type, turned round and shot Mr. Stenhouse dead. This really pissed off the good folks of Edinburgh and a riot proceeded, only brought to an end when the Froggie was hanging from the end of a rope and was also very much dead.

The French made Leith their base and set in for the winter war. The war with England began to go the Scots way and Edinburgh remained secure with the English forced to stay in their garrisons. By 1549 the English were stuck in their self-made prisons. The French treated the English with the respect they deserved and ignored them.

The Froggie's placed an army at Jedburgh a nice base in the borders were they could make little shopping trips into England, buy a few pressies then kill the shop owners as well as the locals. As for Somerset things were not going to well in England and he was sacked. England was in deep shit, financially she was broke. Her new Protector was a chappie who went by the name Earl of Warwick, he was forced to face the facts and throw in the towel.

Henry II of France was cock-a-hoop; being a little bit on the cocky side he was now sure he could get his Frog paws on England through Scotland. In September 1550 Henry threw a party at his joint to celebrate his recent victories, the bash was held at Rouen.

The main guest was the bird that was Queen Mary's mother, Mary of Guise. She arrived with a group of her best buddies. It was at this do that Mary got to see Mary for the first time in two years.

Henry truly believed he would soon be King of England, Scotland and France, thus the wee Queen was a very important pawn.

In 1554 Mary of Guise took over the jobbie of Regent. However there was another problem in Scotland, Protestantism had begun to spread. The Reformation was in the making. A group of chappies formed themselves into a mob known as the 'Lords of the Congregation.' These blokes had a Covenant drawn up in December 1557. They soon found out that their ideas were favourable to others. Meanwhile plans were well in front for the marriage of hairy Mary to the French Dauphin (why, she was marrying a bloody big fish I've no idea). Before the two kids got hitched, Mary was kindly asked to put her mark on three secret documents.

Mary was perhaps too young or thick to realise what she was doing. This was to prove the first of Mary's many political fuck ups.

The Roman Catholic Church had been abusing its position for years. The teachings of the dudes Martin Luther and Johnny Calvin appealed to many seeking religious fulfilment, or to put it another way they were beginning to realise what they could gain for themselves out of it. The wealth of the church that had a few bob was to be redistributed. Most Scots especially those living outside the main towns were happy and jolly enough to stick to their old faith. They knew only too well, the new faith would guarantee one thing, trouble. Trouble there was indeed, it all flared up in 1559, there was a Protestant uprising.

Mary of Guise had her arse kicked out, she was overthrown and Edinburgh was taken. At Leith there was a newly arrived French army and they were ready for some serious butt kicking.

Henry II of France had kicked the bucket. Queen Mary's new hubby now took on the jobbie as King of France. Being a cheeky wee git, he also proclaimed himself King of Scotland. The French had now pushed their luck too far. The Scots decided to end the 'Auld Alliance.'

Mary's mummy Mary dropped dead of dropsy in June 1560, the claims and the ways of the house of Guise died with her.

In 1560 the Reformation took hold and Scotland became a Protestant country. Mary who was a Roman Catholic didn't give two hoots at first. Then in December her hubby was no longer 'here.' He died of the one thing every woman is guaranteed to give her hubby, earache! He died of a septic ear.

With her hubby no more, Mary was about as popular as her hubby's earache to them. It was time for Mary to get her arse back home and govern her own Kingdom.

Froghead made her trip home in August 1561. She landed, having avoided the English ships which had been sent out to capture her. She landed in thick fog at Leith. She was escorted to the Palace of Holyrood. When she arrived at her new digs she heard singing. She looked out the window and at first she though to herself, ah that's nice, the locals have come out to welcome their Queen. Then she felt like she had just dropped the hair drier in the bath! She realised that the crowd gathered outside were singing psalms; this was their way of telling her to fuck off back to Froggieland. This was a shock she was never to fully recover from.

The Catholic Queen now knew she was about as welcome as a bad dose of piles. Mary had an uphill struggle on her hands. One man in particular was to do his utmost to make her life hell. He was a dude who went by the name John Knox. Mr Knox was born in the boring little town of Haddington, also the birthplace of the famous cannibal, Suanny Bean, a man who really knew how to get his teeth into his subjects, but he was of strong English stock. Knoxie did his learning at St Andrews University. When he was 16 he learned of a hot chap, who was burned as a Protestant martyr, a dude who had went by the name Patrick Hamilton.

On learning of Hammy's fate, Knoxie a man full of hate, was even more determined that the Protestant faith would take hold. In 1536 he was ordained a priest. He didn't take the jobbie as priest, instead he decided to con people so he became a lawyer.

He became matey with a chappie who went by the name of George Wishart. Wishy had come back to Scotland with a few mates of his. They were shit-stirrers trying to press ahead an Anglo-Scottish alliance.

Knoxie took a fancy to this English agent and stood by him tooth and nail. In March 1546 Wishy had totally pissed off a dude who went by the name Cardinal Davy Beaton. He was a chappie who was a firm believer in the French alliance. Mr Beaton's favourite pastime was burning Protestant's. Beaton had the hot-headed Wishy burned at the stake. By this time the peed off Protestants were getting a little fed up with Davy burning their mates at the stake. A few weeks after the frying of their man Wishy, the Protestant chappies went round to have a wee word with Mr. Beaton. They invited themselves in, grabbed Mr. Beaton round the throat and told him he was about to get some of his own medicine. To this he replied 'You cannot kill me I'm a man of the cloth.' The Protestants agreed and Davy was placed in a barrel of brine and pickled. The reformationists fair chuffed with the pickling of Beaton took control of St Andrews Castle.

Over the next few years they were joined by many mates including codmouth Knoxie.

This group of reformationists were awaiting help from England. They received different visitors altogether. In July they fell under attack from French troops. Some got in the way of the odd cannon ball and were blown to bits others said 'sod this for a game of soldiers', stuck their hands in the air, and were captured.

Amongst those silly enough to be captured was Mr. Knox. He was put on trial and found guilty of being a naughty boy. It was decided that a nice little cruise might help change his ways of thinking.

He was sentenced to 18 months chained to the oars of a French galley (that will teach him for sticking his oar in!). He was released at the beginning of 1549, after his time working as a deck hand he needed a wee break, so he popped off to England for a holiday.

At this time England was ruled by Edward VI, he was the grand old age of 12. Being of such a respectable age and having a mind of his own, he was being raised by the Protestant party, a fact that suited Mr. Knox very well. Knoxie was doing well for himself in England, but he wasn't daft. He worked out when the 'always puking' young Eddie puked his last; he would be succeeded by his half-sister Mary. Her hobby was also setting fire to Protestant's. Indeed when she did come to power, she went on to get a tally of nearly 300 Protestant's torched, including five of Eddie's bishops. Her motto was simple, if you're going to have a bonfire do it in style. So when Mary took the jobbie as English Queen in 1553 Knoxie did a runner, he bolted off to the Continent. He spent some time in Frankfurt-on-Main, but decided to be frank with himself and thought, this is not the main place to be. He moved on to Geneva, there he got matey with some other English who had also done a runner.

He met a dude who went by the name Johnny Calvin. Boxy Knoxie was fair taken with Mr. Calvin's teachings on the dude Christ. In 1555 he felt it safe enough to come back to bonnie Scotland.

It had been five years since any heretic had been put to flames. Knoxie's timing for leaving had been spot on because as soon as he had left his effigy was burned.

Mr. Knox had a long hard think about the folks who were the most against the Protestant's. Being a fair-minded chappie he soon worked out who was at fault, the answer was simple, of course was… women, it was their entire fault.

He set about attacking any women's right to rule. He put quill to paper and wrote a pamphlet stating his case, 'The First Blast of the Trumpet Against the Monstrous Regiment of Women.' His lovely little book was released in the spring of 1558.

Near the end of that year Mary of England wasn't feeling too well and crocked it. She was succeeded by her sister Elizabeth I (also known as 'white-puss' by her mates), Lizzie wasn't all that hot on the idea of burning Protestant's, so the bonfires were halted.

The Protestant's in England were jumping with joy, knowing they could now jump out of the frying pan without ending up in the fire! Mr. Knox however had fucked up; Lizzie was none too happy with his anti-women book. So Knoxie was about as welcome in England as a butcher on a vegan's picnic.

Lizzie's coming to power gave the Scottish Protestant's more balls. The revolt in Scotland was by now a lot closer. Knoxie came back to Scotland and within six weeks it was a Protestant country. He became Minister of Edinburgh. He was one mean dude, full of hatred. Especially for women in power, he also had no time for Roman Catholics; Mary Queen of Scots was both!

Mary being boss demanded the right to hold mass in her chapels (never heard them called that before). This really pissed off the Protestant's and chappie's like Mr. Knox. Mary did not make one move against the Protestant Kirk. Even despite the fact that Knoxie, who was as about subtle as a sledge hammer over the back of the head gave her a good stiff talking to.

Mary with hubby no more, needed a new man in her life. She was a no-bad looking lass with a few bob in the bank, therefore a good catch. There is no doubt that Mary was a very remarkable bit of stuff. She was a lass with a fair bit up top and could read in six different lingo's including Greek. Her future hubby was going to have to be something very special and indeed he was. He was a one off, a pathetic lanky creep.

He was a dude who went by the name Henry Stewart, Lord Darnley. He was born in England in 1545 brought up there; he grew to be a lanky wimp. Darnley arrived in Scotland in February 1565. Like Mary, he also had a claim to the English throne and if these two got it together, it would enhance their claim. The miss-match of the 16th century was in the making. Mary fell head over heels in love with Mr. Darnley, she decided to get hitched to him.

When the news broke, Lizzie of England went fucking bonkers. John Knox being the reasonable chappie he was, decided the marriage was just about as bad as the end of the world. He was no having it, this was a dangerous Papist union. An interesting fact, but Darnley was himself most likely a Protestant!

The two cousins got it together and tied the knot at such speed that there wasn't even time for a quick fart, everyone was taken by complete surprise. It only took Mary a few weeks to suss out what kind of man her new hubby was, an immature, weak and impulsive prick.

He was a brutal ambitious creep who was not fit enough to be her consort, let alone King, apart from these minor faults he wasn't that bad a guy.

Mary, needing someone to turn to, started to get closer to her musician-secretary. He was an Italian dude who went by the name Dave Rizzio. He was a merry gay chappie, who had by this time got right up the noses of all the big-shots. They were kind enough to class him as an arrogant interfering upstart.

As for the Protestant's they had made up their minds that Mr. Rizzio was a Papal spy.

Queen Mary's buddy was not a popular bunny; what's more he knew it. Darnley full of hate and jealousy, hatched a plan to rid the Queen of her newfound friend. He got together with some other dudes who were not overly keen on the Queen, and were about to have their properties removed by the state.

Darnley did a sneaky deal with them. They give him a hand to do Rizzio in and he'll kindly give them a helping hand in the future. Darnley wanted to receive the crown matrimonial, which of course meant that if Mary popped her clogs he would become King. The first part of his plan was to get rid of Rizzio, the Lords gave their backing to the first part of the plan. On the evening of 9th March 1566 the Lord Morton made sure all roads to Holyrood Palace were blocked. Darnley and his new found pals, who included the disgusting Ruthven placed themselves in the Palace. Mary was having some nosh in her private quarters when the door burst open. Rizzio being a brave eyetie calmly jumped up and down, he screamed for Mary to help him, he knew he was in for one hell of a kicking. Mary was not at all happy that she had been disturbed while having her din-dins was held at bay. Mr. Rizzio was pulled by the hair into the next room. There he was given a good seeing too. Darnley and his buddies got their point over and stabbed Rizzio 56 times. Rizzio did what all good eyeties do when they've been jibbed 56 times, he died. Another reason why Darnley had this crime carried out in front of the Queen, was most likely the fact that Mary was six months up the stick. Being the sick minded git he was, he believed that Mr. Rizzio had been having it off with his wife and was the Daddy and not he. There is not the slightest bit of evidence to back up Darnley's way of thinking, in fact he almost certainly was not the Daddy because he was a well known horse's hoof!

Mary did not miscarry as was hoped and she gave birth to Darnley's kiddie, the future James VI three months later. The day after Rizzio's murder Darnley held his promise to his mates, he discharged Parliament and the Lords got off the hook. The Earl of Moray, who made sure he was nowhere near the scene of the crime the night before, rode into Edinburgh feeling smirk with some of his Protestant chums.

Mary was now in the hands of her Lords and some fast thinking had to be done. She smiled and said she forgave them and bygones were bygones. Mary then talked her hubby into fleeing with her to the castle of the dude Jimmy Hepburn, Earl of Bothwell, his joint was at the lovely sea-town resort of Dunbar.

All the while she had been gathering support against the rotten sausages that had cut her favourite musician to pieces. When they clicked on what was happening, the murderers decided it was time to take a little holiday and fled to England.

Moray and his chums got out of Edinburgh faster than a rat up a drain-pipe and the delightful Mr Knox, who was in full favour of Rizzio's demise, fled to the West Country.

Within 10 days Mary went back to her house in the Capital with her head high. Darnley of course, promised the Queen that he himself had nothing to do with the murder. This was soon disproved as he was grassed by his mates who were in on the murder. Lord Darnley had done himself no favours. Not only did he now have no friends, but everyone also had a reason for having him done in, he with good reason, was now a very worried bunny.

On 19th June 1566 Mary dropped a kiddie, her son Jimmy. She gave birth at Edinburgh Castle. It is believed by some that Mary's kid was still born. As that would fuck things up a little, the dead child was placed in a hole in the wall in Mary's room.

The child was swapped for another, said to be that of the Countess of Mar. This child was raised as James VI. Certainly James was to prove very different to the rest of the Stewarts. More interestingly in 1830 the skeleton of a newly born child was found in the walls of Mary's room in the castle. It was said to be wrapped in the robes of Mary. It was placed back and restoration work was completed. In 1956 it was found again, once again it was said to have been placed back in the wall.

Only this time it was said not to be the bones of a small child, but the bones of a rabbit! A Masonic rabbit at that, today it is known as the mystery of the 'Hole in the Wall'

In December Mary had her kiddie baptised by Catholic rites. Thus led to the belief by some that a Catholic revival was on its way. Darnley by this time had become one heck of a pain in the arse for Mary.

The problem of Darnley was soon enough solved. Here lies one of the greatest 'whodunits' of all time. The murder of Queen Mary's second hubby Lord Darnley.

Mary found him utterly repulsive and beyond doubt had prior knowledge of his murder. Darnley had no been keeping too well, his illness unknown but most likely syphilis, he was in Glasgow when he first started to feel poxy. Mary decided to bring her sick hubby back to Edinburgh and she found digs for him in a house at a place called 'Kirk O'Field' just inside the walled city. Mary at this time would have appeared to have had a change of heart towards her hubby. She visited him and even stayed a couple of nights in a room under his. Darnley was starting to show signs of improving and it was looking likely he would be moved to Holyrood Palace.

There were many people who had no desire to see him back at his wife's side. One chappie in particular had a very good reason to make sure Darnley never returned to his misses. He was the Earl of Bothwell Jimmy Hepburn.

He was a no bad looking dude with lots of balls what's more he had been giving Darnley's wife one behind Darnley's back. More to the point Jimmy thought the Queen had a bun in the oven and that bun was his!

On the night of the 10th February 1567 Edinburgh shook from a great explosion. The 'Kirk O'Field' was blown up into tiny bits. It was not however the explosion that killed the Queen's 20 year old hubby, for he was found very much dead in the garden with his servant who was also very much dead.

There wasn't a burn or a bruise on them, they had both been garrotted. Mr Bothwell was brought to trial for the murders, but a few back hander's took place and Jimmy was acquitted.

Within three months of hubby number two's murder, Mary took on hubby number three, none other than Jimmy Hepburn 4th Earl of Bothwell. His climb to power was proving successful, at least for the time being.

The Earls may well have put up with the Queen having Bothwell as a bit on the side, but there no bloody way they were going to accept him as King!

Mary was beginning to lose the plot as well as mates, by the kind folks of Edinburgh she was classed as a whore.

The nobility decided it was time to kick arse, they put together a bunch of guys to sort the Queen and Bothwell out.

Mary's third marriage had led her into one thing, one heck of a lot of shit. All this led to the punch up at Carberry Hill near Musselburgh. That is; the punch up that never was. It took place on 15th June 1567.

On one side were Mary and her latest hubby. On the other side was the army of the very pissed off 'Lords of the Confederates'. Their boss was the dude who went by the name Jim Douglas, Earl of Morton (also known as 'keep yer heed on Jim' by his mates). Queen Mary was told they had no quarrel with her, but her hubby Jimmy was getting it. She was told in no uncertain terms to dump him. The two sides got chatting and tried to work things out rather than killing each other.

They even came up with the wonderful idea of a hand-to-hand punch up between a champion from either side. However while most of the gibbering was going on, most of the Queen's army had buggered off.

Mary stuck her hands in the air and surrendered to the 'Lords of the Confederates'. Bothwell, showing he had bottle, bolted from the scene faster than an Aberdonian leaving a bar when it's his round.

First Jimmy went to Orkney then on to Shetland, still no feeling safe he moved on to Norway. The Norwegians no taking any of his crap threw him into prison. It is said that this was for ditching a bird there a few years before.

He was moved about prisons for a few years, and ended up in a lovely little pad in Denmark. Dragsholm Castle there they treated Scotland's King with the respect he deserved. He was chained to a wall in the dungeon for 14 years. He died totally off his trolley, a raving lunatic. Today his remains are one of Denmark's oddest tourist attractions. Mary was first taken to Edinburgh and from there to the castle at Lochleven. On 24th July she was forced to give up her jobbie as Queen. Her wee laddie was to take on the jobbie as King, with Moray taking the jobbie as Regent.

A short time after she was forced to abdicate, she also suffered a miscarriage of twins. Moray found himself in a tricky position when Mary managed to escape from Lochleven on 2nd May.

Surprisingly she still had enough mates to raise an army. This led to the punch up known as the battle of Langside, which took place near Glasgow on 13th May 1568. The scrap that took place was not all that impressive. Moray wanted no great shedding of blood, especially his own. The casualties were slight, the odd guy got a belting. Mary's army of about 6000 took to their heels.

Mary now decided it was time for her to do a runner herself. She fled to Dundrennan then across the Solway to the Kingdom of her cousin, Elizabeth of England.

Mary stepped ashore in England only three days after getting her arse kicked at Langside. Her arrival caused great embarrassment. Mary a Catholic queen in a land that was ruled by a Protestant queen, whose nearest relation was Mary.

Miss white puss of England had some tough decisions to make. Within five months Mary was in the scenic town of York and on trial. She was charged with crimes against Moray regime.

The main evidence against her was the now infamous 'Casket Letters', which were no doubt forged by Moray and Morton. All this led to one thing Mary was to stay in England at her cousin's pleasure, and Moray was to go home and get on with the jobbie of being Regent.

Moray carried on with his jobbie until one day he was silly enough to get himself murdered by the Hamilton's. Lord Darnley's Daddy got the jobbie as Regent but he too was silly enough to get himself murdered.

Mary now a queen without a Kingdom was kept prisoner in England for 18 years. There are many stories about Mary's plots to overthrow her cousin Lizzie. The story of Mary can go on forever, like all monarchs she had her good points and her bad points. She was a good-looking lassie who had an eye for the boys. She is even alleged to have had a string of toy-boys. A good looking dude would be brought to her in the evening. She would spend the night with him most likely playing cards or the like. In the morning the young dude would be taken out to the garden, asked kindly not to say anything to anyone.

Then to make sure he kept his gub shut he would have his throat slit. He would then be thrown over the wall and left for the crows to peck at!

The English themselves prolonged Mary's life by keeping her under arrest. They kept her in nice clean digs keeping her away from all the nasty diseases of the day.

When it was finally decided that Mary's Frog head was to be removed from her shoulders, it was Mary herself who signed the order.

It had been noticed that she signed her official papers without bothering to check what she was signing. Her death warrant was slipped in. Mary signed without checking the small print.

At the age of 44 Mary was taken to the great hall of Fotheringhay Castle. She faced her execution on 8th February 1587 with great ease. It took the big bad dude with the axe only three times to chop her head off. When he finally managed to get her head off, he picked up the head to show the crowd what a clever chappie he was. As he raised the head higher he found suddenly that he was only left with the wig!

Mary's head fell from the wig and bounced off the ground. Mary Queen of Scots was buried at Peterborough Cathedral; she was later to be reburied at Westminster Abbey. James VI (also known as 'tin-roof' to his mates) took on the jobbie as King at the mature age of 13 months. James was brought up and taught by the great George Buchanan, Buckets took great pleasure in thrashing the King and telling him what a nasty bit of stuff his mummy was.

Mr Buchanan was about as nice as a rusty nail in the foot, but he was also one of the greatest scholars of his day. James was taught so hard that he himself reckoned he could speak Latin before he could speak his own native Scots!

Scotland was as usual ruled by Regents while the kiddie King was growing up. The last of these Regents was Jim Douglas, Earl of Morton. Mr. Douglas was the strongest of the Regents. He held power from 1572-1578.

He was a chappie who ruled in his own manner, which meant he was as popular as a poke in the eye.

'Keep Yer Heed Jim' introduced to Scotland the 'Maiden', a beheading machine. In 1578 he was removed from power by the Earls of Atholl and Argyll, in December 1580 at the age of 63 he was arrested by King James for his part in his Daddy's murder.

He was found guilty and was asked if he preferred to be hanged or beheaded. He replied 'It makes no indifference to me; I'll be deed either way.' Morton had his head cut off on his own beheading machine.

It was a clever device in which the blade was raised to a certain height. The blade which had a lead weight on it would then be dropped on to the neck of the unfortunate chappie. It would be dropped at such speed. It would only take two to three drops before the head was completely removed from the body.

After Mr. Morton's head was cut off he was quartered, then a different part was placed above each of the gates of Edinburgh for public display. The all-powerful Douglas family nagged the King for the return of their beloved Jim. They wanted the pieces back so they could bury him.

After six months the King said ok you can have the bits of the body but not the head that stays were it is. The four parts of the body were removed from their poles and buried. The Douglas mob still kept nagging James for the head, after two years since he was beheaded the Douglas's got their own way and was allowed to remove the head from its pole.

They were so chuffed at getting his skull that they placed it on a silver tray and took it to St Giles Cathedral. There they all stood round the birdie poo skull and sung songs to it. The skull was then taken to the Greyfriars Kirkyard and buried beside the other parts of his body.

At the age of 14 James fell in love for the first time, his first love went by the name Esme Stuart, a first cousin to the King's Daddy. This wee poof arrived from France in 1581 and James had the hoots for him big-style.

He soon made Esme Earl of Lennox and a privy councillor. The nobles were cheesed off with all the special treatment that Mr Stuart was receiving. It was soon decided that Esme was a Papal spy! Esme's downfall was in the making.

James was out playing er, I mean riding with some of his very Protestant mates. They decided to give the King new lodgings for a wee while.

James was kidnapped and held captive in Ruthven Castle. It was there he was to spend many an unhappy hour, until he escaped 10 months later.

However the damage was done and James's very close bum chum Esme had been forced from office. He fled to France were he died in 1583. Never forgetting his love for the young King of Scotland, he left James a little gift in his will. His embalmed and broken, heart!

James was now starting to rule by himself, as well as ruling he was fair keen to put quill to paper. He was an intelligent King, but a King scarred by his upbringing.

There had been nine attempts to kidnap him in the past. James ruled as a King suspicious of everything and everyone. He never ever overcame his fear of strangers. He thought of them as nasty chappies who might stick a large pointed thing into him, so in precaution he wore thick padded clothes.

He had all the standard problems with earls and nobles always wanting to kick each others heads in. As well as this there were punch ups between the Protestant's and the Catholic's James just shrugged his shoulders and let them get on with it.

If you were a good looking young chappie you would stand a very good chance of getting a good jobbie in his court. King James was to grow into a man who had a taste for the finer things in life. He was also a man full of hatred for the nastier things in life, such as witches. James had to be a good Protestant and stay on good terms with his cousin Lizzie of England. If she kicked the bucket without an heir there was a good chance that her Kingdom would become his Kingdom.

In 1587 when Lizzie had James mummy's head cut off, he merely made a small protest saying it was a bit rude to cut one's mummy's head off.

He decided in 1589 to go for a wee holiday to Oslo, while he was there he might as well pick himself up a wife. He found a lassie that went by the name Annie of Denmark.

On his way the sea crossing had not been a pleasant one and the ship nearly sunk.

James being a man of intelligence and logic knew the bad crossing was the work of one thing and one thing alone, witches! Scotland's history of witchcraft rates amongst the worst in Europe, the chappie most responsible was non-other than King James himself.

James decided it was the nasty witches who had plotted to stop him returning from Denmark. The witches had tried all manner of things, such as toads, wax dolls and spells which included the use of royal underwear.

When these didn't work they tried experimenting with charmed cats held by the tail and swung three times round the head anti-clockwise. Then they were thrown into the Forth to conjure an almighty storm that would sink the King's ship!

King James was told of the entire peculiar goings on. He was horrified and not a happy bunny. More than that he became obsessive and as a result most of those who were unlucky enough to be accused of the nasty goings on, suffered hideous torture and an agonising demise.

These folks became known as the North Berwick witches. A lassie who went by the name Euphemie MacKalzane was one of the lucky ones, she was only barbecued alive, and another Agnus Sampson got a slightly better ending she was strangled before she was set on fire.

One lass who went by the name Barbara Napier claimed she was up the kite. When James heard this, he ordered his physicians give her the once over. To check out if she was telling porkies or not. If she was telling fibs then she was to be disembowelled then publicly thrown into a fire.

Over 100 poor souls who were lucky enough to suffer in the North Berwick witch trials. The most famous was the dude who went by the name John Cunningham. His daytime jobbie was a school teacher, he was fortunate enough to have both his legs crushed in a device called the 'Boot.' Then he was tied to a stake and cooked.

The dude that caused the biggest upset was a chappie who went by the name Ritchie Graham. Before he was done in he started to gibber all sorts of names. He really put the cat amongst the pigeons when he claimed it was none other than the Kings nutcase of a cousin Francis Stewart, who was the main man and masterminded the whole rotten business.

Francis Stewart was a well- known bad egg; one example of his matter was on the 30th July 1588. Mr. Stewart was walking down Blackfriars Wynd in Edinburgh when he bumped into a dude who went by the name Sir William Stewart.

It was well known that these two guys didn't exactly see eye to eye with each other. A quarrel broke out and Mr. Stewart used colourful language to Mr. Stewart. Mr. Stewart got a little bit upset at this and used even more colourful language back.

Mr Stewart then drew his sword, on seeing this Mr. Stewart placed himself up against the wall. At this stage of the proceedings Mr. Stewart run his sword right through Mr. Stewart in such a way it entered in his back and came out at his belly. To this Mr. Stewart said 'ouch' and dropped dead.

Pleased he won the quarrel Mr. Francis Stewart went on his merry way.

The implication that Francis was in on the nasty stuff gave King James all the excuses he needed. Francis got his wrist well and truly slapped he lost all the privileges a dude of his rank could expect in those days.

So being a heeder he went to war with the King, but it wasn't much of a scrap and never amounted to anything. He managed to escape the flames and was exiled to Italy were he burned himself out in 1613.

King James had such a fear of the supernatural that he even wrote a book on the subject in 1597, his bestseller was called 'Daemonologie.'

Witchcraft in Scotland became so horrific that tales relating to it can make yer spine curl. The story of the Balfour family is just one such case. They were taken from their home in the Orkney Isles in 1595. In Edinburgh they were showed the sights like the castle, they were then horribly tortured for the crimes of witchcraft.

The youngest member of the family, the daughter who was just seven years old had the 'Thumbscrews' placed on her. These were placed at the base of the nail, thus being the most sensitive part. Then they were tightened and tightened until the thumb was about to explode.

The son was placed to the 'Boot', the iron boot was placed round the calf of the leg at such an angle, that when large wedges were hammered in. The foot was crushed until the blood spurted out, not only the blood but the very bone marrow itself.

The mother was placed in the vice, with the vice the hands were tied round the back at such an angle that when she was raised to the ceiling her shoulders were dislocated. Then large weights were tied to her feet and she was left hanging there for three days and three nights. However they were kind enough to light a fire under her feet, to keep them warm!

The father was pressed to death, with pressing you were tied to a rack. Then a large board was placed the chest. Weights were added one at a time, till the final weight was added and the entire ribcage would collapse inwards, piercing the very body organs themselves and this was only one family! Between 1479 and 1722 sixteen thoussnd witches were put to death in Scotland.

Early in the morning of 24th March 1603 old white puss Lizzie, 'pussed away'. This was the news James had been waiting for, he was like a kiddie with a new toy he was chuffed right down to his royal bits. He was awoken in Holywood Palace and told his cousin was no more, at this news he jumped with joy and shouted 'oh goodie.' The consequences for Scotland were momentous. In the spring of 1603 James packed his royal bags and was off to his New Kingdom, England. There he was boss and he ruled as James VI & I.

He liked his new found wealth and even toyed with the idea of uniting Scotland and England into one Kingdom, Great Britain. However the Scots were no for thrusting their big next-door neighbour, who had been trying to get their paws on Scotland for hundreds of years. There was no way James idea was going to happen in his lifetime.

He now ruled Scotland by pen as always he had the problems of the Highlands was the clans did things their way. James dealt with this by issuing powerful letters, which allowed clans to kick the neighbour's backsides, if they were out of order!

He was proving to England that he was in charge of the Highlands; he made an example of the Clan Macgregor. They were to suffer terribly all their lands were taken from them. Their very name was removed and made illegal. Many Macgregor's got the shit kicked out of them.

The MacDonald's of Islay also had their arses well and truly kicked. The King's own cousin a dude who went by the name Patrick Stewart, from the Orkneys. King James was kind enough to have him strung up in front of a large group of spectators.

In 1608 a few of the chiefs were invited on to one of the King's ships, for a wee bit of a do and a wee chinwag to sort things out. Instead once they got on the ship they were all arrested and chucked into the clink. The following year after they had all promised to be good boys and behave themselves, they were released.

On the condition they also sign a bit of paper stating they would now do things James's way.

In 1617 fourteen years after he had left his native land, James decided to come back for a wee break. James by this time was far from popular with his forgotten people.

What's more he was about to impose his 'Five Articles.' These were simple little things like Holy Communion will be received kneeling. The festivals of the Christian year will be observed, bishops would administer confirmation and not by ministers, only in the case of serious illness would Private Communion be allowed.

James knew what was best, he was the King so he was damn well going get his own way or else. In 1618 the 'Five Articles' were pushed through. They were about as popular as a bacon sandwich to a Jew.

Most would rather walk for miles than take Communion in a 'kneeling church.' By 1624 James wasn't keeping to well and his laddie, Chas with some help from one of his Daddy's very good buddies took the reins of power. In 1625 James pooffed off to the sky, with him no more, he was succeeded by his midget son.

Charles I (also known as 'Pratt heed' to his mates) came to the throne 27th March; he was born in Dunfermline in1600. Chas was the last Scottish King to be born in Scotland.

Chas' growth had been stunted by rickets, so he grew to the tall height of 4ft 9in. He was a wee chappie with big ideas. Chas was never meant to be King, that jobbie was reserved for his big brother Henry but he didn't fancy the jobbie much and decided typhoid was much more fun, he stuffed it at the age of 16.

Chas was the first in a long line of absentee monarchs. He left Scotland as a sickly kid in July 1604. He had been left behind when his pa-pa got the jobbie as King of England. It was 15 months after his old man left before Chas was well enough to travel. Chas did not have a good family upbringing, his Daddy caring more about his boyfriends than his own laddie.

In 1625 as well as taking the jobbie as King, he got himself hitched to a Froggie bird, a Catholic lass who went by the name Princess Henrietta Maria.

Chas was chip of the old block, just like his dad he was a devout Anglican and Episcopalian. He believed that he and he alone was right. He had no time for what he knew of the Kirk and Presbyterians.

Chas fully believed that since he was only answerable to God, it was his jobbie to bring the Scottish Kirk into line with the Church of England. Thus he set forth to do. He soon started to lose mates big style.

He upset a bunch of dudes who were known as the 'Lords of Erection' these fine upstanding men who did their job hard-on, he was most likely trying to help, when he brought in his 'Act of Revocation' in 1625.

Things started to go pear-shape and he ended up being mistrusted by all. In 1629 being the boss he demanded that all religious goings on in Scotland conform to the way of the English. Chas was now as popular as reindeer-steak at Christmas!

In 1633 he made his way back to Scotland for the first time since he left 29 years before. He came back to what he called 'Our ancient and native Kingdom.' He was to be crowned by a dude who went by the name Billy Laud. Chas had given this guy the jobbie of Archbishop of Canterbury. The coronation was held at St Giles Cathedral in Edinburgh.

Chas was given the full works, candles, crucifix, genuflecting bishops and of course the full Anglican rites. Edinburgh was made a bishopric and St Giles was now a Cathedral. Needless to say this went down like the Titanic.

There was now only one word on the lips of the men of Scotland 'Popery.' Pratt heed and his new Archbishop carried on and mucked things up even more. Then they put their heads together and managed to work out that the English Prayer book in its present form could never be accepted in bonnie Scotland.

Therefore they set about doing a 'Revised Prayer Book' for the Scots. This book was read for the first time in St Giles on 23rd July 1637. The good folks of Edinburgh being a reasonable and understanding lot. Listen to the first few lines then picked up their stools and started to chuck them at the minister.

Fists and boots were flying all over the joint and it didn't take long before Edinburgh was engaged in a full-scale riot.

Chas was in London at the time and couldn't give a monkey's shit about Scottish affairs. On hearing what had happened he simply sent word back. Saying all that had protested against the Prayer Book, were to have their butts kicked. The regular use of the book was to be enforced.

In Scotland all the bigwigs were getting a fed up with Chas crap, they started to get together in their opposition to the book. As for Chas he was clueless to the hornet's nest he had opened.

Chas got nothing but complaints about the book, every time he got a complaint he merely issued orders for the moaners to be kicked-in.

At the Mercat Cross he had a paper read out telling everyone to shut their faces and start doing what they were told, by the one who knows all, their King. This time Chas boy had pushed his luck too far.

The group of dudes who called themselves the 'Lords of the Congregation' got together again for a get-together.

On 28th February 1638 Greyfriars Kirkyard in Edinburgh was the in place to be. This was the meeting place of hundreds of folks, bigwigs to poorwigs, they were all there for one good reason. They all wanted to make their mark on a document which had been drawn up.

This document was to become known as 'The National Covenant.' From Greyfriars copies of the Covenant were sent out to all the Burghs and Parishes for the flock to stick their mark on it.

Some of the more fanatical nutter's even signed it in their own blood! The 'National Covenant' was in fact the first true form of democracy, because it didn't matter whether if you were skint or loaded you were still able to sign it.

What the Covenant was stating was stuff the King's authority up his royal arse and while you are at it you can stuff Parliament's authority to boot. The people could look after themselves.

They wanted a Parliament that was not answerable to Chas. Most folks didn't want to start a massive punch up. All they wanted was things to be the way they were before Chas stuck his oversized oar in.

The Covenant was also a confession of faith, pledging support for the Protestant religion. The 'Covenanters' as they would become known all had one thing in common they were all fanatical nutters. They were answerable to one person and one person alone, that person was the big man himself, Mr. God. The Covenanters claimed it was not the King himself they were pissed off with but his advisors, especially the bishops.

Chas being the ever reasonable chappie decided the Scottish Covenanters needed a good boot up the arse. He wouldn't be able to raise a Scottish army so decided an English one would do the trick.

However when he put his plan into action he was shocked to find the English weren't too chuffed with his idea. Most English sympathised with what the Scots were trying to do.

What's more the Covenanters were sure that God was on their side, so there was no way they would ever lose not to an English army or to their King.

In 1639 Chas was once again ready to kick Scottish nuts. His main army would cross the Tweed and make their way to Edinburgh. At the same time a naval force would land lots more troops from the Firth of Forth.

Chas was a happy bunny at his cunning little plan. Unbeknown to him the Covenanters had plenty of spies in the King's court. They knew full well what he was up too. They decided to go for a picnic to the Borders and meet the Kings mates.

Chas soon found out he was up against a formidable mob, his bottle soon crashed when he realised he didn't have enough guys to take on the Scots. Thought the matter over decided to be a nice King for a change, he offered a compromise.

The 'Treaty of Berwick' offered peace, but was unlikely to offer a lasting peace. Chas being a two-faced git offered peace only for one reason and that was to get some time to get his act together.

He wanted to build up an army that could kick the Covenanters up their religious bums. In 1640 he set about doing this, but as usual the Covenanters spies were spot on and had full knowledge of the Kings plans.

In England things weren't all that grand either Charles had problems with the English who were getting more and more pissed off with his stupidity.

The Covenanters in Scotland couldn't keep their lads on the Border forever, waiting for Chas to invade. Their answer to this little problem was simple. They decided to force Chas hand by invading England.

By doing this they were chancing their mitts and taking one hell of a gamble. How would the English feel about being invaded! The Covenanters set about letting the English know they had nothing against the English or did they wish to break the 'Union of the Crowns.' So please be kind enough to be good chappies and stand aside while we invade your country!

On 20th August 1640 the mob of the Covenant went on a wee stroll to England, their first meeting with the Kings army on 28th amounted to no a lot. The Kings army was led by a dude who went by the name Lord Conway, he had stuck in at school and wasn't too bad at the old arithmetic and soon realised he was outnumbered. He and his men filled their pants with a smelly substance and did a runner.

Mr. Conway's lads were expected to fall back into Newcastle, but instead they kept on running and left Newcastle to fend for itself.

The army of the Covenant took Newcastle without kicking anyone's head in. Chas was by now losing his authority with his English subjects a well. The Covenanters were over the moon and knew he would soon come round to their way of thinking.

In October 1640 the 'Treaty of Ripon' was drawn up. The Scots were to keep Newcastle and the surrounding areas for themselves, until Cha came up with a peace deal.

The Scots knew full well he was a lying toad, so they made conditions to make sure he kept his word. No doubt the one that got up his nose the most was that he had to pay the Scottish army a wage while they were occupying part of England! The 'Bishops Wars' were over.

They had took on the King and called his bluff. In 1641 Chas went to Edinburgh and set about destroying his own power over the Church of Scotland, doing away with the bishops in favour of a Presbyterian system. As well as having to do this Chas also had to hand over most of his power to the Scottish Parliament. He was now no more than a figure head in Scotland.

The Covenanters were now chuffed to bits. They had achieved their revolution against what seemed impossible odds. Their victory was short lived. The 'Bishops Wars' had set a cat amongst the pigeons all over Britain.

In Ireland the oppressed Irish Catholics took to arms, (why did they no take up legs as well?) This was seen as a threat to the Scottish settlers in Ulster. In 1642 a large Scottish army was sent there for some good old butt kicking.

In the same year England went to war with England, the King and the English Parliament were now engaged in a full-scale scrap.

In 1643 the Scots decided the best way of protecting their revolution was to send another Scottish army for a wee vacation in England, and give the English Parliamentarians a helping hand.

By this time it was obvious that Chas had only made concessions to the Scots in 1641 so he could work on beating up his English enemies. Once he had dealt with them he would deal with the Scots.

The Covenanters moved into England and managed to get themselves up just about everyone's noses. Within a short time they would give the English the excuse to invade Scotland.

In 1646 Chas now knew he didn't have a hope in hell of winning the English 'Civil War' however he still held on to the fact that he was the boss and had the divine right to be an absolute ruler.

When the war was at its beginning the English weren't slow at offering the Scots whatever they wanted, if they would help to kick the King's butt. Now that the war was nearly over they changed their minds and were now most unwilling to help the Scots.

The Covenanters by this time were pissed off with English lies and started to wonder if Chas, now that he had his wrist well and truly slapped would be worth talking to.

Chas was soon up to his old tricks and hoped to play the Scots off against the English. In hope that in order to outbid each other, one would do a deal with him.

In April 1646 the Parliamentary armies were closing in on him, if didn't fancy being captured it was time to do a runner. Chas who was in Oxford dressed himself up as a humble servant and with a couple of mates he slipped out of the city and made his way to the Scottish army headquarters at Newark-on-Trent.

The Scots surprised by their new visitor made Chas as welcome as a caterpillar in a salad! He was made a virtual prisoner. The Covenanters were like a dog with a new bone, they now held the main card and if they played it well the rewards would no too bad.

They took Chas with them back to Newcastle, so they could think of the best way to get their way. The Scots soon found that Chas was about as much use as a hole in the head.

He was just no playing the game and wouldn't help in any way whatsoever. What's more the English were going bonkers with the Scots for trying to do a deal with the King.

They threatened the Scots, telling them the way they were going they were going to get a good bashing. The Scots now found themselves in a bit of a pickle, on one hand they had Chas who was as stubborn as a mule and wouldn't make any concessions. On the other hand the English were getting very cheesed off with them for still being on English soil, after the war had ended.

The Covenanters now had the problem of getting rid of Chas without losing face at the same time. The way around this was easy, as the Scots withdrew from England. They left the King behind his Scots guards, then buggered off and abandon him.

At the same time he was grabbed by English Parliamentary guards, this of course was nothing more than a pure coincidence!

The Covenanters however had not handled matters well before they left England, they demanded that they receive some of the back-pay they were due. The English parliament was nice enough to hand over a wee bit of dosh, £20,000. To some it looked like the Scots had sold their King.

On returning to Scotland the Covenanters discovered that all was not well. By getting rid of Chas the way they had, brought about a resurrection of royalist feeling.

By 1647 the Covenanters were split into two factions. One mob wanted to renew contact with the King. So they got pally with the moderate royalists, and it was this group of chappies who won control.

Being in charge they opened up a chat-line with the King, who was imprisoned at Hampton Court. Chas was to head for Scotland if he should escape. Being a clever bunny he did escape, then did his usual and fucked it up. Instead of Scotland he ended up on the Isle of Wight!

He was once again chucked into prison. The Scots keeping their hopes alive once again made another deal with him. This was called the 'Engagement', the Scots would work hand in hand with the royalists to get the King free and would even be kind enough to lend an army if the need be.

In the summer of 1648 the Scots squad marched into England to help their buddies the royalists. But the royalists were busy getting their arses tanned, the Scots ended up in a punch up at Preston.

The English Parliaments army was led by a dude who was making a big name for himself in England, Oliver Cromwell (also known as 'wart's he all about' to his mates).

Mr. Cromwell treated the Scots army with the same respect he had shown the royalists armies and totally crushed them.

With the army of 'Engagement', disengaged and their faces smashed in, their regime in Scotland fell to pieces. The extreme Presbyterians of the Kirk party, who hated the 'Engagers', now, grabbed power.

They made promises to Ollie that they would be of no trouble to England. This of course just wasn't true some already had big ideas on imposing Presbyterianism on England.

Ollie Cromwell gained control of England but he still had the wee problem of Charles I to deal with. Thus he did by putting Chas on trial for starting a second civil war and bringing in foreign invaders, the Scots.

Chas was now charged with high treason and up to his neck in elephant poo-poo. The Kirk party launched their objections and made one hell of a noise telling Mr Cromwell hewas just not on. Mr. Cromwell said he was on and the King was put on trial.

The Scots were horrified at the position they were now in. If Chas boy was executed they would have to make his laddie, King of Scotland, but he would not be King of England as England would be a Republic.

They would also for the fact no be happy with England for executing the chappie that was in fact ruling the country next door. The English slung a deafie on the Scottish protests and Chas was found guilty.

Chas was to have a hair cut from the neck up, his head was to be chopped off. Before he was decapitated he had one last request, a simple one. He asked that his head be sewn back on to his body after it had been cut off!

The reason was simple he wanted to be whole and complete on the day of the 'Resurrection.' His request was carried out and some poor git had to spend hours sewing the Kings head back on to the King!

On a freezing cold January morning in 1649 Charles I was no longer head of state in fact he longer had a head. His head was cut off by a big man with a big sharp axe. One swift stroke of the axe removed the head of the King of Scotland and England.

The Scots on hearing the news were not overly chuffed and straight away proclaimed Charles son Charles as King.

Charles II (also known as 'Bignose' to his mates) was King of Scotland and England.

But Mr. Cromwell was now in charge of England and he was going to get things his way.

First of all he sorted the Irish out by crushing them in 1649.

Ollie now turned his yaks on the Scots. Charles was asked nicely or else to sign the Covenant, thus he did. Cromwell was now as loony as a man with a ferret up his trousers and sent his troops over the Scottish Borders.

In July 1650 wart-face came to Scotland with one or two mates, 16,000 to be exact. He also sent a fleet sailing up the east coast for some extra support.

Ollie wanted to meet his fleet for a cup of tea. However he soon found his way was blocked by a dude who went by the name Davy Leslie, his daytime jobbie was boss of the Scottish army.

Cromwell was forced to withdraw to Dunbar; he was now like a kid who had just had his sweets nicked. At the beginning of September Mr. Leslie went to Dunbar to ask Mr. Cromwell, just what the fuck he thought he was playing at.

The Scots squad now numbered 20,000. They had a great view of the seaside resort as they were massed on Doune Hill, looking doon over the toon.

The Scots army had Ollie by the balls. All they had to do was sit tight starve Mr.Cromwell and his cronies out. But the ministers who were about as bright as a blackout, started to lead the Scottish troops down the hill to meet the English for a punch up.

The experienced English army couldn't believe their luck, at the stupidity of the Scottish ministers. As a result they kicked many a head in and over 3000 Scots were slain, another 10,000 were taken to new digs called a prison.

The Kirk Party as well as the Covenanters now got themselves together and an unbelievable royalist's revival took place. The Scots using the crown as a symbol of resistance to the invaders from over the Border, the auld enemy.

Charles I was now enjoying popularity, but by now it made no odds because he was potted meat!

The Scots were in a hopeless position and in desperation decided to invade England.

This was to prove not one of their better ideas as Charles II army at Worcester was destroyed. They got a right sore doing.

Scotland to all intent and purposes was now a conquered country. Ollie now showed what a nice understanding chappie he was. In place of the 'Union of the Crowns', Mr Cromwell imposed an 'incorporating union' which meant the Scottish Parliament was abolished.

After the punch up at Worcester Charles and some of his mates did a runner overseas.

Scotland was ruled by Cromwell until he popped his warts in 1659. Two years after Cromwell stuffed it, the English decided to put him on trial. They had a slight problem; he was well and truly dead and buried!

This problem was soon solved, they dug him up. The corpse was put on trial and found guilty; he most likely used his right to remain silent! He was taken from the court and hanged, two years after he had stuffed it. His skeleton remained on public display for 12 years.

With Mr. Cromwell no more Charles came back and took his throne (were he took it to I've no idea). His homecoming was not the best of news for the 8th Earl of Argyll; this guy had been crawling up Ollie's arse. For being nice to Cromwell he was put to a simple death, he hung drawn and quartered. His head was placed on a high pole for all to see for 12 years.

Charles II having no great love for his Scottish subjects never bothered to visit Scotland again. For the next 25 years he governed Scotland through a 'Privy Council' as had his Daddy and Granddaddy.

The Privy Council was based in Edinburgh, while its secretary was over 400 miles away in London.

Charles who signed the Covenant in 1649 was not in the least bit interested in it. He had only signed to secure his Coronation and he didn't give a monkey's hoot for what he had agreed to do.

He set up his Privy Council without any reference to the Scottish Parliament. Like his Daddy he was a two-faced so and so. He was going to do things his way; he was going to do as his Granddaddy did. This of course meant that he himself would choose the 'Committee of Articles.'

This tightened his position with Parliament. The church soon realised they were back to square one.

A covenanting minister, dude who went by the name Jimbo Sharp was packed off to London with the jobbie of Emissary to the Court of the moderate Presbyterians.

He did his jobbie so well he came back with a new jobbie! He was now Archbishop of St Andrews and professing entirely different opinions from those with which he had set out with. Some of ministers weren't over keen of doing things the King's way, so they started to do things their way. About 300 of them got their act together and buggered off from their manses and churches. It wasn't long before they were holding unauthorized religious services.

In nice homely places like empty barns and bare windy hillsides, the Privy Council being the understanding chappies they were, soon got pissed off and started to impose fines.

This of course meant one thing, more people were about to get their noses broken. The group of dudes who were holding these meetings went by the name the 'Conventiclers' (I don't think I'd like a kick in the Conventiclers!).

In 1663 a chappie who went by the name Sir Jim Turner was sent out with soldiers to beat up the Conventiclers. The Conventiclers on hearing the news that Turner and his boys were on the way, stopped getting together for praying and started to get together to form a squad.

All these guys wanted to do was pray but if anyone was going to try and stop them they were more than willing to kick their teeth in.

In 1666 the punch up known as the Pentland Rising took place. Sir Jim Turner considered himself a bit of a hardnut and on 13th November a group of his mates were kind enough to impound some corn in lieu of an unpaid fine.

The local laird and his buddies weren't too happy about having their corn nicked. So they set about nutting the soldiers. As soon as the locals heard there was good punch up on the go they rallied together with the laird and his mates to beat up the soldiers.

This group of dudes having enjoyed themselves so much, they decided to march to Dumfries. It was there that they found the dude who had really peed them off, Sir Jim himself. They made him their prisoner.

The conventiclers had a bone to pick with the Privy Council and they were going to get their say or else.

A small group of them about 1100 set off for Edinburgh armed to the teeth with deadly weapons like scythes, pitchforks and staves. The weather was kind to them with the rain pissing down and the winds freezing the balls off them.

By the time they got to Edinburgh they were knackered. They were chased to the Pentland Hills and made themselves comfy at the base of the hills.

It wasn't long before the government mob made their way there to give the Conventiclers a kick in their peculiars. They made their stand but soon realised that this was not one of their brightest ideas.

Before long, about 50 of them had been planted. Under the cover darkness most of them decided to do a runner back to their homes. About 80 of them were not very good at the old running game and were captured.

The government took an understanding point of view with these dudes, 21 of them were hanged. The government stuck their foot down and resorted to even tougher repression. Anyone who hanged about with the Conventiclers was to be hanged.

This didn't stop these chappies, in fact their meetings started to spread and they held mass meetings. By 1674 the Conventiclers, were building up their strength again.

Many were captured and given a new home on the Bass Rock, this big lump of rock on the Firth of Forth was the new state prison. The government crapping themselves in case of a rebellion asked the Highland Clans to be nice kilted chappies and lend some support.

On 26th December 1677 a commission was issued for this. On 24th January to big tough Highland laddies were ready to go on their little holiday and march from Stirling to Glasgow.

They were put to good use. These guys knew how to knock someone's pan in. When they withdrew they left behind many a skint and bitter landowner. These measures however did not reduce the size of the mobs and the Conventiclers were now drawing crowds of up to 14,000.

The pot really started to boil over on 3rd May 1679 when the dude Jimmy Sharp, Archbishop of St Andrews was ridding along merrily in his coach. A bunch of nasty angry men jumped the coach and gave Mr. Sharp the sharp end of their swords. Sharp got the point and died.

On the murder of the Archbishop the Privy Council set out even more determined to curb the Conventiclers. The Conventiclers were now themselves split amongst the moderate and extreme chappies.

The most extreme was a dude who went by the name Rab Hamilton. He was one of the guys that done in Jimmy Sharp, he published his intent to revolt at Rutherglen on 29th May 1679.

The Privy Council answer to this was to call on a dude who went by the name Johnny Graham of Claverhouse. Claverhouse was no mean dude he set out with a group of mates in search of the rebels. In May he was in the wee toon of Hamilton, it was there he managed to get his paws on the dude John King.

Mr King was one the bigmouth field preachers, if he had something to say he said it. Claverhouse caught him with 14 of his sidekicks. Mr. Graham was on a bigger high when he heard that there was even more Conventiclers nearby at a place called Drumlog.

Claverhouse jumped on a bus and made his way to the marshy moorland and decided to kick butt. The Conventiclers didn't fancy the idea of getting their butts kicked, so they kicked butt back, a good butt kicking session was to be had by all.

Mr. Graham not liking a sore butt had to withdraw. He was also silly enough to have lost a few of his officers as well as 30 of his mates. The insurgents were like a guy who had lost a penny and found a pound they were now on a high and tried to take Glasgow.

They failed, so they established their main camp at Bothwell Bridge a joint no to far from Hamilton. Their army grew in size (they must have been eating their porridge) but so did their fall outs.

Declarations and counter-declarations, which were to prove important for both Presbyterianism and the Covenanting cause were made, from all this bickering emerged two main parties.

One of these was very clerical in its leadership and was made up with most of the 18 ministers in the insurgent army. This group of dudes wanted to work under a free General Assembly and keep on the right side of Charles II.

The other group of dudes led by Mr. Hamilton stressed they were far from happy with the King and were unlikely to be in the near future. All the fun of their debates was brought to an abrupt end on the 22nd June.

A dude who went by the name Duke of Monmouth and who was also the bastard son of Charles arrived on the scene. For good measure he brought some chums with him an army of 5000 government troops.

Mr. Monmouth and Mr. Graham let the punch up commence. The government troops got tore in; they out numbered and out gunned the disorganised Covenanters. The scrap was over in no time at all, about 200 lay spattered on the field. 1400 stuck their hands up and said 'take us, we're yours.'

Mr. Monmouth was in a good mood and favoured clemency and a new 'Indulgence' was issued in September. As for the chappie Johnny King he was put on trial with another chappie who went by the name Johnny Kid. King and Kid were both hanged for being naughty boys. Another five dudes were also hung for refusing to admit they knew anything about the murder of Archbishop Sharp.

As for the chappies who were captured they were given new digs in Greyfriars Kirkyard in Edinburgh. As a reward for getting themselves captured 258 of them were transported.

They were placed on a cruise liner 'The Crown of London', for their comfort they had balls and chains placed on them, other words 'manicalised.' This however was not very helpful, when the ship sunk off Orkney taking them with great speed to the bottom with her!

The Covenanters may have had their arses kicked, but they were still stubborn as ever.

The 1680's went down in history as the 'Killing Times' and for a good reason.

At the Mercat Cross in Sanquhar a dude who went by the name Richie Cameron made his stand. Being a preacher he opened his big gob and publicly called for his mates to rise to the occasion against the King and his government.

Those who were silly enough to listen to him all met various unpleasant ends. In 1685 the last King to be crowned in Scotland stuffed it. He was succeeded by his wee brother.

James VII & II (also known as 'Honest Jimmy' to his mates) came to the throne with something that wasn't very popular with his subjects, he was a Roman Catholic.

He was the first Catholic on the throne for over a hundred years. Jimmy had his head in cloud cuckoo when he tried to include his co-religionists into the main jobbies of power.

He was a little under sensitive to say the least. Jimmy was born in London in 1633; he was the second laddie of his Daddy Charles I. Before his pa lost his heed, Jimmy was raised as a Protestant.

During the Civil War the Parliamentary forces captured him, but he managed to do a runner and escape to Frogland. He like the joint so stayed there for 12 years having an extended holiday.

During his time over-the-water he made a name for himself (mustn't have liked the one he had) in the French and Spanish armies. He went back to England in 1660 when his brother got the jobbie as King.

Unlike Charles Jimmy was unable to hide his religious preferences, thus making him about as popular as a dragon with flatulence! He didn't help matters when he got hitched to wife number two, a bird who went by the name Mary of Modena and just happen to be an Italian Catholic.

The shit really hit the fan in the summer of 1688, when Mary finally gave birth to a male heir after 8 miscarriages. Many never wanted an heir to be born. The thought of a Catholic male heir scared them witless. Rumours were rife. Things like, the queen was never up the kite in the first place. Instead of having a bun in the oven she in fact had a cushion up her dress!

When the kiddie was born they even went as far to make up stories, saying he was a changeling who had been smuggled into the royal bed inside a warming pan! Before long panic was in the air and a conspiracy was formed.

An invitation was sent to Jimmy's son-in-law a poof who went by the name Willy of Orange (also known as 'creep' to his mates). Willy was hitched to Jimmy's lassie Mary, more importantly he and she were

Protestants.

The invite was for Willy and his missies to come over to England and restore Protestant liberties. Willy quite fancied the jobbie as King and came straight over. On his arrival Jimmy decided to do a runner to France, he took with him his other half and his wee kiddie. The kid now went by the name Jim Francis Edward Stewart. He was to go down in history as the 'Old Pretender.'

In April 1689 Willy and his wife Mary took on the jobbie of King and queen together, he taking the jobbie as King she taking the jobbie as queen. On reflection the jobbie of queen would have been much more suitable for Willy. He was as bent as a nine bob note.

James VII short rein was over he ended his years a sad and bitter old git, he made a couple of attempts to get his throne back. The first one was made in Scotland in 1689 by the good dude Johnny Graham Claverhouse, who had by now earned the loveable name of 'Bluidy Clavers', for his ruthless pursuit of the Covenanters. Now he had changed sides and was fighting for his mate Jimmy.

A few days after Willy and Mary were proclaimed King and queen, Claverhouse raised the royal standard on Dundee Law. Claverhouse was no longer 'Bluidy Clavers' but the first Jacobite commander. He was now known as 'Bonnie Dundee.'

He had to raise an army if he was to have a go at Willy, so decided on a wee break to the Highlands. The Highland Chiefs were the only ones who could help Dundee, but he would have to win them over first.

Lucky for Dundee he had the gift of the gab and some spare dosh to offer. He soon got the Chiefs round to his way of thinking. Dundee raised an army and spent three months building it to strength.

While he had been doing this William II & III had made a dude who went by the name Hughie MacKay of Scourie his General. MacKay was a chappie who had been born in Sutherland, but had grown to dislike the Highland way of fighting. MacKay led his buddies to meet Dundee's army for a chinwag.

On 27th July the two sides met at the narrow pass of Killiecrankie. Dundee had a mob of 2500; MacKay had a mob of 4000 and two cavalry troops. To get his point over he also had three small cannons and 1200 packhorses.

On hearing reports that Dundee was on his way to give him a kicking he cared not.

The track through the pass of Killiecrankie was narrow and ran near the river. Being one of the more modern tracks in Scotland it was wide enough for three men or one packhorse at a time.

Thus the dude who went by the name Farquhar MacRae and who was a dab hand at the old sniping game hindered the advance while Dundee's army did a bit of hill bagging and raced up the hill.

The two armies faced each other from the two hill tops did the usual waving at each other then bared their arses at each other, this went on for two hours. At 7pm they decided to charge at each other and kill as many of each other as possible.

The Jacobite army was not in the best of moods and cut MacKay's army to pieces.

Such was the destruction of King Willy's army that their blood flowed over the heather like waves of red water.

Dundee led the charge of the Highlanders and he survived the main battle. When the punch up was nearly finished Dundee did a rather silly thing and wandered in the way of a stray musket ball. The ball struck him and rendered him from breath.

One tale tells the story of Dundee's death and in fact could well be true. During his life he upset quite a few folks some even believed he was a 'Warlock.' It is even said that his horse a black charger was called 'Satan.' The horse was said to have been a personal gift from Old Nick himself!

In fact his death is said to have been caused by a silver bullet. (A coat button!). A few years before the punch up of Killiecrankie, while serving his time as rounder upper of the Covenanters, Dundee had a curse placed on him by a bird that went by the name Mrs Brown.

Dundee wanted to arrest her hubby; he refused so Claverhouse shot him dead. Mrs Brown being a little pissed off by this cursed Dundee. She vowed that Claverhouse would know 24 hours before he was about to die and a silver bullet would finish him off.

The records show that the night before Killiecrankie Dundee was restless and couldn't sleep, it is said he acted very strange that night. He knew of his impending doom. He was kept off the field as much as possible during the battle. The battle was all but over when he was hit by a stray shot from nowhere. Said by some to be a silver bullet, said by others to be a 'coat button.'

The Jacobites won the day, but at a high cost 900 of their men as well as Dundee lay dead. MacKay's army was slaughtered. He fled with just 400 men. The battle is best remembered through the song;

> Whare hae ye been sae braw, lad?
> Whare he ye been sae brankie, O?
> Whare hae ye been sae braw, lad?
> Cam ye by Killiecrankie, O?
> An ye had been whare I hae been.
> Ye wad na been sae canty, O;
> An ye had seen what I hae seen,
> On th' braes of Killiecrankie, O.
> I faught at land, I faught at sea;
> At hame I faught my auntie, O;
> But I met the Devil and Dundee,
> On th' braes o'Killiecrankie, O.
>
> If ye had been whare I hae been,
> Ye wad na been sae canty, O;
> An ye had seen what I hae seen,

On th' braes of Killiecrankie, O.
The bauld Pitcur fell in a fur,
An' Clavers gat a clankie, O;
Or I had fed an Athole gled,
On th' braes o'Killiecrankie, O.

Without a leader the Jacobite campaign fell to bits. Six weeks after the Battle of Killiecrankie, King Jimmy was on holiday in Ireland. It was there that he got involved in a little punch up, the Battle of the Boyne.

He walked away with second prize. Jimmy went back to the land of the frogs. His chances of getting his crown back were in tatters.

Jimmy during his lifetime, like most of his ancestors was shall we say was very friendly with the ladies. In his final years it is said he paid and died the price of his over-indulguence. He caught the 'clap', Syphilis.

In his last years his mate Louis XIV who held the jobbie as King of France allowed Jimmy the use of a spare house of his. The Palace of Saint-Germain-en-Laye a joint near Paris.

This pad became the home of the Jacobite Court for nearly 25 years. Jimmy went to meet his maker in 1701; his heir to the empty throne was his laddie Jim.

After Killiecrankie Scotland was a split nation. The Highlands in favour of Jimmy the Lowlands in favour of Scotland's first foreign King, Willy.

As for Willy himself he had a great dislike for the Scots, whether they be Highlanders or Lowlanders.

William and Mary recognised the Scottish Government. The following jobbies were given to the following dudes. The zealous Presbyterian Earl of Crawford was made president of the estates. Lord Melville was made Secretary of State.

Viscount Stair was made president of the Court of Session; his son who went by the name of Sir John Dalrymple got the jobbie of Lord Advocate. The Duke of Hamilton became Lord High Commissioner to the Estates. This group of dudes were to play an important part in Scotland's history.

In England Willy was being pressed to opt for Episcopacy in Scotland. In Scotland Melville was in full favour of Presbyterianism. Willy knew full well that the Presbyterians were never likely to support James, so he allowed them to get their way.

As far as he concerned the pacification of the Highlands was a matter of urgency. A new fort was built and named after him 'Fort William.'

In May 1690 a group of warships flying the flag of Willy of Orange, sailed the Western Highlands. They contained two things, one, 800 government troops and two, enough materials to build the new fort at Lochaber.

The main dude behind the scheme was the chappie Hughie MacKay, whose arse was still sore from the kicking he got at Killiecrankie. At first he didn't travel with the troops, he decided to stay in the safety of

Edinburgh Castle.

From there he planned his next move. On 3rd July Mr. MacKay got his act together with 7000 of his buddies and went to meet the ships at Loch Linnhe. Work on the new fort started right away and within 11 days the first part was complete.

Hughie named it in honour of his King. The garrison to keep the Scots at bay was built. It was besieged with problems over the years and never achieved much except giving the town of Fort William a much-detested name!

In 1691 a commission was given to the dude Johnny Campbell of Glenorchy, the first Earl of Breadalbane to bring the Highland Chiefs to the King's loyalty. He was given £12,000 pocket money to help him do so. The 'Massacre of Glencoe' was in the making.

In June there was a massive get together in a castle that was falling to bits. The meeting took place at Achallder on Loch Tay. There were 500 big hairy Highlanders there to meet Johnny and hear what he had to say for himself.

He brought all the Clansmen together to let them know a wee idea of his, which he thought would bring peace to the Highlands.

Mr Breadalbane wanted to raise a Scottish militia for King Willy. As some encouragement the English Parliament offered £12 grand in bribes. Johnny would give the dosh to the Clans, so they could use it to purchase free title on their lands.

In return the Clans just had to one small minor thing. Take an oath of allegiance to King Willy, who at the time was busy having a war with Louis XIV in Flanders.

The Highlanders would of course also be expected to raise a standing army (why was he no wanting them to sit doon!) to give Willy a helping hand in France.

The Highland Chiefs being ones for a quick buck and being fast thinkers took three weeks to make up their minds. The decision was a hard one, but they finally agreed to the plan.

Mr. Campbell was cock-a-hoop and he set off to London where he gave his news to Queen Mary. Then he took a boating holiday to Flanders to tell King Willy that the problem with the Highlanders was no more. Mr. Breadalbane was known by his enemies as 'Cunning as a Fox' and not without good reason, as the Macdonald's the traditional enemies of the Campbell's would soon find out!

On 17th August 1691 King Willy signed the order telling his Highland subjects to take a binding oath of loyalty to him. It had to be subscribed to before 1st January 1692. Being a nice King once it was signed he would reward them by restoring the Chiefs ownership of their lands. The Highland Chiefs were told in plain language sign this or yer getting it. If they didn't sign they would suffer the severity of the law.

By this time the Chiefs has lost all faith in Johnny Campbell. The Master of Stair Johnny Dalrymple wanted the Highlanders dealt with and would have been quite happy to see them put down like dogs.

King James sent a message from France to the Clan Chiefs telling them they must do whatever they must for their own safety. The postal system in those days was a wee bit on the slow side and the letter didn't arrive until the 28th December, three days before the deadline.

The dude who went by the name Alasdair MacIain held the jobbie Chief of the Glencoe Macdonald's. On reading the letter Mr MacIain set out immediately to take the oath on behalf of himself and his men.

He went to Fort William to sign the oath and have a quick pint. But he had buggered up as the order had to be signed in the presence of a sheriff. The nearest sheriff was at Inveraray 60 miles away.

A nice dude who went by the name of Colonel Hill was kind enough to give Mr. MacIain a letter to take over the hill with him. The letter said that Alasdair had been a silly prick and had gone to the wrong town. Armed with this letter and in shocKing weather conditions MacIain set off for Inveraray.

But when yer luck's oot its oot. MacIain was arrested by grenadiers from Argyll's Regiment. Being fair-minded chappies they decided the letter was a fake and held Alasdair for 24 hours, 24 hours to long!

When he finally got to Inveraray the deadline had passed and to make matters worse the sheriff had buggered off. He did however return on the 5th January. Being the grumpy git he was he refused the oath at first. Ally knew he was he deep shit if he couldn't give the oath, so he nagged the sheriff till he took it.

The oath and letter were forwarded to Edinburgh. In Edinburgh the lawyers refused to accept responsibility for an oath delivered late. The result MacIain's name was struck from the record.

Stair was like a cat in a mouse factory when he heard the news. Breadalbane was now in full favour of force instead of talk. King Willy of Orange and so-called King of Scotland signed the order for the elimination of the Macdonald's of Glencoe.

In charge of the action was a dude who went by the name Colonel Jim Hamilton. The agent was a pathetic piss-head who went by the name Captain Rab Campbell, when he was sober he was cousin to Breadalbane.

Stair let it be known that the operation was to be 'secret and sudden.' In those days Highland hospitality was everything, you never asked but if you did you were given it whether friend or foe. The plan was to ask for digs and food and in return kill the hosts.

Two companies consisting of about 70 men set out led by Glenlyon. Alasdair was surprised by their arrival and was a wee bit unsure of them, but what he to fear he had signed the oath.

For 12 days MacIain and the Macdonald's wined and dined them. They let them billet in their homes. Whether Glenlyon knew of what his orders would contain is unknown.

What is known is that when he got them they were very explicit.

His orders came, it is said by some written on the playing card 'nine of diamonds', that card to this very day is now known as 'The Curse of

Scotland.'

The orders read 'You are hereby ordered to fall upon the Rebels, the Macdonald's of Glencoe, and put all to the sword under seventy. You are to have a special care that the old fox and his sons do upon no account escape your hands, you are to secure all the avenues that no man escape. This you are to put in execution at five o'clock precisely.'

Glenlyon would block all escape routes to the south. Another dude who went by the name Duncanson with 300 of his best mates was to block the mouth of Glencoe. Mr Hamilton was to block the east with his buddies.

There were 850 fully armed men with the given jobbie of wiping out 500 men, women and kiddies. The fateful deed was carried out in the early hours of 13th February 1692.

The guests attempted to do their hosts in as they had a kip. Things did not go to plan. Mr. Hamilton never reached the east held up by the good old Scottish weather. Mr Duncanson it would seem without an excuse was also late.

By this time the Macdonald's had cottoned on to what was going on. Most of them managed to escape through the snowstorm. There were not fast enough on their feet to avoid a slaughter. MacIain himself was murdered trying to do up his trews as he got out of bed. One of the Campbell soldiers decided to get his teeth into Lady Glencoe; he used them to rip the rings from her fingers.

The killing was indiscriminate and ruthless anyone who was unlucky enough to be caught was slaughtered on the spot. This included one 13-year-old kid who was unfortunate enough to run into the path of Captain Drummond. Mr. Drummond took great pride in gunning the lad down. A six year old clung on to Glenlyon's trews and begged for mercy, it was not given.

All prisoners were executed. The time morning light had come 38 Macdonald's lay butchered in the snow, about the same number also perished in the storms as they tried to do a runner. One of the worst chapters in Scottish history had taken place.

When the news of Glencoe broke Scotland was shocked to the core. This was a horrific event even for those hard times. The public kicked up fuck for justice and the Government was forced to hold a commission of inquiry.

Three years later the inquiry found Stair guilty of causing the massacre. He merely shrugged his shoulders and said he had only been doing his jobbie! As for King Willy he was not in the least bit interested in the whole affair, he cared not. William was now as popular as an elephant farting in yer face.

Under the 'English Navigation Act' goods could only be landed at English ports by English ships. This caused Scotland dearly it blocked the way to expansion overseas, in days when expansion was a necessary.

The Scots were pissed off with England pissing on them; it was now time to take matters into their hands. In June 1695 a project was launched o try and give the Scottish merchants a better chance against their English competitors, who were getting everything their own way.

Disaster was in the making. The Scots decided to establish a colony where the isthmus of Darien joins central to South America. This was a desperate measure by desperate people, an ambitious plan, but just plain stupid. It was ill thought out and doomed from the start.

Scotland despite the 'Union of the Crowns' was denied access to England's ever growing empire. The Scots had also been dragged into Willy's punch up with France. This war was ruining Scotland's trade on the Continent. They would have to go much further to do sell their gear.

Out of all of this was born the 'Company of Scotland Trading to Africa and the Indies.' King Willy was not a happy bunny; he was not in favour of this at all. But it was only three years after Glencoe; feelings were still high so he gave his approval but only just.

The new company soon found they were to get no help from London. The Scots then went a joint called Amsterdam. They enjoyed the nightlife and were on a high, while there they looked for some backers. They soon found that Dutch Willy had let it be known that they were to receive no help. The Scots were up the creek without a paddle. If they couldn't get help from London or abroad they would have to go it alone.

Anyone with some dosh to invest did so in a burst of patriotic fever, they were sticking the finger up to England.

The Scot behind the plan was a dude who went by the name William Paterson he was a chappie from very humble beginnings. He had made a hell of a lot of dough for himself as well as a good suntan while trading in the West Indies.

Mr. Paterson really laid on the patter in London were he formed what is now known as the Bank of England. Bill never forgot the land of his creation and he wanted Scotland to prosper. His dream for years was for Scotland to have her own colony in Central America.

In early winter 1697 the ships were lying ready in the Firth of Forth. The 'Caledonia' the 'St Andrew' and the 'Unicorn.' They were loaded with everything needed for a wee holiday in the jungles of Central America. Simple things like booze, beer and brandy and a few of the non-essential things from needles to axes. To be on the safe side they decided to take some food with them.

In July 1698 they were off, the small fleet set sail on the high seas. Crowds lined the harbour as well as nearby hills to cheer them off. The ships were at sea when one of the sailors with a sharp eye noticed that most of the food on the 'Caledonia' was no good for man nor beast, rotten meat and mouldy biscuits (why does that remind me of the wife's cooking!). Grub that was meant to last nine months would now be lucky if it lasted six months.

The passage itself was no clever, choppy seas causing many of the soon to be settlers to be a little unsettled, they puked their load non-stop. When one threw up over one's mate it often caused a fall out, before long misery on the ships were rife.

A couple of months after leaving, they arrived in the West Indies. Bil Paterson who had gone along for the fun of the journey set foot ashore He was lucky enough to bump into a dude who knew his way about, he was an old buccaneer. He kindly led them to a sheltered inlet.

Things were no easy and problems were mounting every day with the daily burials of victims of fever and lack of breath. The Scots put much thought into giving their new home a name. They came up with the great original name of 'Caledonia.'

Led by Captain Drummond of Glencoe fame, they started to build a fort. It was hoped the fort would give them protection against the expect ed attacks from the Spaniards. The Spanish were no happy bunnies with the Scots setting up a colony in what they classed as their territory.

The Scots were now living in a hutted settlement, which once again they used all their brains to name, it was called 'New Edinburgh' things go bad to worse, rations were low and Saturday night fever was big.

Then came the rain, coming from Scotland they thought they knew what rain was. They were well wrong. The settlers were by now in a pathetic state with no strength to have a brawl with the Spanish when they came.

Being strong and determined chappies there was now only one option and that was to do a runner and the settlement was abandoned.

The ships made course for Jamaica the 'St Andy' was abandoned own ing to the small fact that her crew of officers and 140 colonists were al deed and buried at sea.

It was just the 'Caledonia' that made her way back to bonnie Scotland The ships had left with 1200 only 300 were making the return journey The fuck up of 'Darien' was only half way. While the colonists were suf fering trying to establish themselves their plight was unknown back in bonnie Scotland.

In Scotland it was the belief that all was going well. A second expedi tion was made ready with an even bigger ship the 'Rising Sun' (I'll bet she was a nippy wee number). On this trip women as well as men were luck enough to get tickets for the cruise. Three ministers were to go along and convert the savage Indians to their Presbyterian way of thinking.

The 'Rising Sun' with her two sister ships the 'Duke of Hamilton' and the 'Hope of Bo'ness' set sail at the end of September 1699. Just 12 days before the directors of the 'Company of Scotland' received word from New York that the colony had been given up as a bad joke.

In November the settlers arrived at their lovely new home. Not the par adise they were expecting but a deserted hell. New Edinburgh was run over with weeds.

One of the ministers was horrified to find the only thing the colonist had left behind was they had taught the native savages a new language swearing!

The new group of settlers was now up to their necks in shit. They were in a desperate position. The huts had to be rebuilt, but there weren' enough axes, saws and their nosh was running out fast.

One dude who went by the name Alexander Campbell decided to have his say and take over as leader, for this he most likely wished he had kept his gob shut as he was hanged for opening his big mouth.

Once again every day that passed had one common element, someone was planted.

Having stuffed it from fever or lack of grub. It didn't matter what came their way they were a hardy bunch. This was their bit of land and they were going to jolly well hang on to it come hell or high water. In the end both came their way.

They sent off some of their auxiliary vessels to seek provisions from the English colonies in the West Indies. On reaching them, the Scots colonists said, 'hello we're in a bit of a pickle and if we don't get some provisions soon we're in deep monkey poo-poo and we'll be six foot under.' They were told 'tough tittie', King Willy had given the order that no matter how desperate the Scots were they were to be refused any help whatsoever.

The Scots colonists were turned away in their hour of need. Things were fast going down hill. Then just when they could have done without it, the Spanish came to knock a few pans in.

The Scots were not going to give up at any cost. Then at long last a dude who went by the name Campbell of Fonab reinforced them, he brought with him 200 much needed buddies.

His army decided to get tore into the Spanish first, and have go at them in their half built fort. They were off to boot the Spanish up the arse. The Spanish put up a good show, but after a few kicks in the nuts they gave way and done a runner.

The Ministers, who should have been chuffed with this victory, were sour face gits and all they did was moan at the soldiers for swearing and being pissed all the time.

The number suffering from fever was now in the hundreds. What's more they were low on ammo.

The dude Campbell of Fonab became nuts and wanted to fight to the last man. He was told to go and jump from a very high tree. The Spaniards offered terms of capitulation.

On 1st April 1700 the Scots finally gave up their cosy little colony. They carried the sick to the ships, held their heads high with colours flying they set off to sea. By the time the ships anchored off Jamaica another 200 had popped their clogs from fever.

Still the English said 'tough tittie', on the orders from the King. A small relief ship from Scotland finally arrived with some help and the ships put to sea. The 'Hope of Bo'ness' got into an argument with some rocks off an island near Cuba, the rocks won and the 'hope of Bo'ness' was beyond hope as she sunk.

The other two ships sailed on to the sunny waters off Charleston, South Carolina.

There they sailed straight into a hurricane. Both ships were lost with all hands the 'Darien Disaster' was now complete.

The results of the Darien fiasco were to have far reaching effects on

Scotland. Scotland now had no love for King William and he for that matter had no love for them. He never ever once set foot in Scotland. His two main interests, one for his English Kingdom the other choirboys and it was this interest that had one good lasting effect, he wouldn't be leaving an heir.

In March 1702 William was out riding his horse, which made a nice change from choirboys. He was hunting for deer when his horse stumbled on a molehill. He was thrown and he dislocated his shoulder as well as breaking a couple of ribs. He died in much pain three days later, much to the delight of the Scots.

To this Jacobites still toast to the 'Gentleman in the black velvet coat', the mole.

Willy was succeeded by his sister-in-law.

Anne (also known as 'Fatty' to her mates) came to the throne in 1702. Scotland in effect had two monarchs, one who held the crown and ruled from London. The other one overseas and who wanted his families crown back, but held no power.

In 1701 James VII & II had stuffed it, leaving his laddie to succeed his empty throne.

James VIII & III (also known as 'nae chance mate' to his mates) had a hard task in front of him.

The Jacobite's wanted to restore James to his rightful place as King of Scotland, England and Ireland. Queen Annie was having none of it, see was Queen and was jolly well going to stay Queen after all she was James VII & II daughter.

Things in Scotland at this time were at an all time low. Scotland was on a downer since Darien. To make matters worse there had been even more shocking incidents of English treatment towards the Scots.

The Scots had to do something to get their pride back, as well as getting on an equal footing with their next door neighbour. When feelers were put out for an 'Act of Unions', there seemed at first there just might be something in it for Scotland.

It has to be remembered Scotland was skint, not a bolt. Bankrupt because of Darien, which the Scots put the full blame on England. This just might be a way of recouping some of the lost dosh.

It would also mean that the Scots could now start to trade on equal terms with their English neighbours. Many of the rich toffs were in favour of the Act, despite the fact that the population of Scotland in whole was strongly against any union with England.

Before a union could go ahead there were some details to be sorted out.

Queen Annie had been quite clever at the old producing kids game trouble was none of her 17 brats were any good at the old surviving game! Thus she had no direct heir. The Whigs in England filled their breeks at the thought of a Stewart getting the throne again.

There was no way they were going to let another Catholic on the throne, hell would freeze over first.

Even though James VIII & III was the rightful King he was not getting the jobbie on any account. In 1701 the English Parliament passed an Act which meant once Annie had croaked her last; the crown would not go to Jimmy but to a German Princess. A lass who went by the name Electress Sophia of Hanover.

Her claim to the throne was the fact that her Grand-daddy was James VI & I. this blocked the way for James to get the throne of England. The English still had to block him from getting the throne of Scotland back. There was one sure way of stopping him getting his jobbie and that was to force a 'Union of the Parliaments.'

The Scots were not slow in the uptake at what the English were up too. In 1704 the Scottish Parliament passed an 'Act of Security.' This simply meant that the Scots would pick their own monarch within 20 days of the monarch stuffing it. It also stated that the successor was to be a Protestant and a descendant of the House of Stuart.

The Act also stated that the successor would not be the occupant of the throne of England. That is unless the English started to play fair and give the Scots equal trading rights as well as equal rights in all manners of Government.

The Scots also placed in it an article which stated that they were free to continue their import of French wine! This was a kick in the hoo-haws at England since England was in fact at war with France.

Queen Annie was advised at first to tell Scots to jump off a cliff. She however had to agree to the Act as she was shitting herself that the Scots might said 'stuff you' and allowed French ships of war to use Scottish ports.

In March 1705 the English came up with a cracker of an Act, this was the 'Aliens Act.' The English Government decided that all Scots were to be treated as aliens with no rights whatsoever, especially when it came to trading.

That was unless the Scots came round to the English way, and accept the Hanoverian succession. It was beginning to look like Scotland and England were heading for one almighty scrap.

The treat of war was brought even closer when in Edinburgh an English dude who had a daytime jobbie as a sea-captain and went by the name Captain Green. Being a little on the greenside he landed his ship at the Port of Leith.

The ship was one of the last surviving ships of the 'Company of Scotland.' Mr. Green was grabbed by a mob, who were far from green with envy but were very much red with anger. Being a fair-minded lot they accused of nicking the ship.

The mob got this one wrong and poor Mr. Green was innocent. But such was the hate for England at the time. The mob wouldn't listen to reason and the sea captain found them a pain in the neck as he was lynched.

War was looking more and more likely. The English Government had enough on their plate with their punch up with France, so didn't want to get into a fight with the Scots.

In the summer of 1705 Queen Annie dispatched a young dude who went by the name Duke of Argyll to Edinburgh. He had made a name for himself fighting for the English in the past.

Mr. Argyll came from a family who had more than once showed their loyalty to the English cause. To this day the phrase 'never trust a Campbell' can still be heard.

Argyll was given the jobbie of talking the Scottish Parliament into talks about talks for a 'Treaty of Union.' After a few beers as well as a few weeks Parliament agreed for the talks to go ahead.

In April 1706 it was off to London for a wee break and some hard talking. Thirty-one mostly Whigs and including the newly created Earl of Stair opened up the talks to thirty-one English Commissioners.

In the gibbering that followed the Scots Commissioners tried to impose a kind of 'Federal Union.' The English were having none of this from the start. It was then agreed that there was to be a combined British Parliament, Scotland would contribute 16 representative Peers.

In the House of Commons the Scottish would be allowed 45 members, the English would have over 500!

Scotland must also accept the Hanoverian succession. In return for accepting this, the Scots would receive 'full freedom and intercourse of trade and navigation.' The real bride was £398,085 that was to be handed over to the Scots with the excuse that it was partly payable for taking share of the English National Debt!

It was also to be partly payable as compensation to the shareholders of the 'Company of Scotland', who had lost all their dosh with the Darien expedition.

Scotland however would still be allowed to retain their own legal system. The emblems of both countries were to be united on one flag, a problem easily solved by placing the St George Cross over the St Andrew's cross.

This treaty was put before Parliament in October 1706. The Presbyterians were of course crapping themselves that an English Parliament might impose an Anglican Church.

Talking soon convinced them that they would be able to keep their Church for the future generations.

With all that done it still seemed unlikely the 'Treaty' would be allowed to go ahead.

The people of Scotland were 50 to 1 against any union with England.

At night-time they would scour the streets and cellars of Edinburgh trying to find the Parliamentarian's, if they got their claws on them. They were going to give them a good hiding and a firm boot up the arse. This was to let them know what the people of Scotland wanted and that was most certainly not a union with England.

The Duke of Queensberry who now held the jobbie High Commissioner came near to copping his lot. The pissed off folks ran after his coach chucking stones at it. Indeed he became a much-hated figure in the streets of Edinburgh. The people on the other hand would cheer at the Duke of Hamilton whenever he appeared on the street, as they believed him to be leading the opposition against the treaty.

Edinburgh was so near to revolt that three regiments of soldiers were called in to keep order. All the while Parliamentarians were meeting in secret, such places as the little well hidden summerhouse in the garden of the dude Lord Seafieid's joint, and now part of Moray House University.

The money on offer was at the forethought of their minds. Edinburgh wasn't the only place unhappy with the goings on; the whole of Scotland was on the verge of revolt.

In Glasgow there was near riot, which ended up with the Provost doing a runner and hiding from in the pissed off crowds in a folding bed!

The time for the voting came and those in favour won the day, Hamilton was not there to vote. He was suffering from toothache. The mass walkout he had said he would lead therefore never took place.

On March 6th 1707 the Treaty met with royal assent and on the 25th. The Scottish Parliament met for the last time. Queensberry made a final speech were he said 'It is full time to put an end to it.'

While he was making his speech, at his house something odd was taking place. On the very day the Treaty was signed. James Douglas, 2nd Duke of Queensberry the 'Iron Duke' took his entire household with him for protection against the angry crowds.

His house was in the Cannongate area of Edinburgh. On taking his entire household with him he left but two occupants in the house. One was a 10-year-old kitchen boy. He was left in the kitchen to turn the spit; on the spit was a roast.

The other occupant was Queensberry's own son. The Earl of Drumlanrig, a giant of a man, a monster. He was a complete lunatic. Drumlanrig had been locked up in the basement for years, for the protection of others.

On this very fateful day he finally managed to escape. The first thing he did was smell the meat cooking. He followed the smell. When the Duke returned it was not the kitchen boy who was turning the spit. It was Queensberry's own lunatic of a son. On the spit was not the roast, but the half-eaten body of the kitchen boy!

Queensberry's house still exists today. For many years there have been tales of a young boy haunting the building. As for Queensberry's house today it has been converted into part of the new living quarters in the new Scottish Parliament, perhaps there's some form of justice in that (now that's the kind of story I can get my teeth into!).

After Scotland was sold away, Queensberry packed his bags and moved off to London.

There he received a pension of £3,000 a year and was given an English Dukedom.

In Edinburgh the 'Honours of Scotland', the Crown, the Sword and the Sceptre were hidden away underground in Edinburgh Castle. The

Jacobites said 'we were bought and sold for English gold' which led to the traditional song of the day. This tells the story of Scotland's death very well;

'SUCH A PARCEL OF ROGUES IN A NATION'

FAREWELL TO A' SCOTTISH FAME,
FAREWELL OUR ANCIENT GLORY,
FAREWELL EVEN TO THE SCOTTISH NAME,
SAE FAMED IN MARTIAL STORY,
NOW SARK RINS O'ER THE SOLWAY SANDS,
TO MARK WHERE ENGLANDS PROVINCE STANDS,
SUCH A PARCEL OF ROGUES IN A NATION!
WHAT FORCE OF GUILE COULD NOT SUBDUE,
THOUGH MANY WARLIKE AGES,
IS WROUGHT BY A COWARD FEW,
95 FOR HIRELING TRAITORS' WAGES.
THE ENGLISH STEEL WE COULD DISTAIN,
SECURE IN A VALOURS STATION;
BUT ENGLISH GOLD HAS BEEN OUR BANE
SUCH A PARCEL OF ROGUES IN A NATION!
O WOULD, ERE I HAD SEEN THE DAY,
THAT TREASON THUS COULD FELL US,
MY AULD GRAY HEAD HAD LIEN IN CLAY,
WI' BRUCE AND LOYAL WALLACE!
BUT ATH AND POWER, TILL MY LAST HOUR,
I'LL MAK THIS DECLARATION.
WE'RE BOUGHT AND SOLD FOR ENGLISH GOLD
SUCH A PARCEL OF ROGUES IN A NATION!

For Scotland the 'Great Wake' had began. The common Scots held a wake. The death being their own country. They took to drinking, for many years over the shame of losing their country. It was from here that term the 'drunken Scot' comes from.

Whether most of those who signed Scotland away believed they were doing the right thing or not are unknown. Perhaps it was the great likelihood of war with England that made these chappies do what they did, but there is no doubt that some only did it to line their own pockets.

Scotland was now ruled from the new British Parliament and it didn't take long before it became oblivious the partnership was far from equal. As far as the English were concerned Scotland was theirs to do as they pleased.

In 1713 a motion was submitted to the House of Commons, that the Act of Unions be repealed. It was of course defeated but only by four votes.

The Jacobites in Scotland had only one hope and that was to get James VIII & III on to the throne. In 1714 Queen Annie stopped stuffing herself and stuffed it instead. The Jacobites hoped for a coup.

The English Whigs were quick off the mark and George of Hanover; the laddie of Electress Sophia was given the jobbie as King, on 5th August. Georgie was publicly proclaimed King in Edinburgh.

There is no doubt that if James had been willing to turn Protestant he would have got his throne and the jobbie of King. Once more Scotland had a monarch who cared nothing for her and to boot this one couldn't even speak Gaelic, Scottish or English!

James gave permission to the Highland Chiefs to honour George I (also known as 'krautie' to his mates) as their King. They sent Georgie an address of acceptance.

Georgie being a reasonable chappie rejected it. Needless to say the Highland Chiefs weren't overly taken with 'German Georgie.' In the Lowlands the wake continued but more and more would raise their glass to the 'King over the water.'

James had tried to come to Scotland in 1708, but the Froggie commander shit himself and filled his pants with smelly stuff when he spotted English ships. He refused to land James, despite his pleas to be landed.

In 1715 talk was rife of another landing. James sent a letter to his buddy, a dude who went by the name Earl of Mar (also known as 'marsbar' to his mates); he asked Mar if he fancied kicking a few skulls in. Could he be kind enough to do him a wee favour and raise the Highland Clans. It was time to bash a few heeds in and get the throne back for the family. Word got out and the very pissed off Highlanders rose for James.

The Earl of Mar had an army of 12,000 men, angry with the union and their rejection by a sausage-eater. With a strong Highland mob behind him Mar soon took Perth.

Between Perth and the Borders stood only 2,000 Government troops. The dude Duke of Argyll led them. Mar when it came to politics was fine, however when it came to fighting he was shite. He was not one bit in the least a military leader.

Perth was his, but being a bit on the clueless side, he stayed there for three weeks missing the very real chance of kicking the shit out of the Government troops. His mob heavily outnumbered the other mob and could have crushed them.

In November Mar heard the news that the Border Jacobites were getting there act together. So he dispatched a mate of his a dude who went by the name Mackintosh of Borlum to meet up with them.

Mr. Mackintosh took with him a couple of mates for company, 2,000 to be exact. He met up with the Border Jacobites and after a few jars they all decided to go for a wee pub-crawl in England. They got as far as Preston, there the English Jacobites fucked things up and Mackintosh and his buddies were forced to stick their hands up.

Mar all the while was enjoying the sights of Perth. In the Highlands a dude who went by the name of Simon Fraser, Lord Lovat and held the jobbie of chief to the Clan Fraser had just returned from a holiday in France. There he had tea and biscuits with King James.

On his return he raised his Clan and promptly seized Inverness Castle, in the name of George I. This little deed put him in the good books with the English. When the Fraser's who had sided with Mr. Mar heard this they decided stuff this and Mar. They buggered off to join their boss with them went many of the Clan Gordon. This was not good news for Mr. Mar and he was now beginning to have problems.

In the North things were not going the Jacobites way and Whig Clans such as the Sutherland's, MacKay's, Ross's, Fraser's and Munroe's were now in charge. Then the news that Argyll was going to get strong back up from Holland. Mr. Mar decided to take his men for a wee walk towards Stirling. When Mr. Argyll heard about this he decided to take his men for a wee walk and see if he could bump into Mr. Mar and tan his face in.

On the morning 13th November the two armies bumped into each other a mile outside a joint called Dunblane at a place called Sheriffmuir. They said good morning to each other then got ready to slaughter each other.

Mar was looking forward to this punch up as he had an army of 10,000 cheesed off Highlander's; Argyll only had 4,000 buddies with him. Argyll lined his guys on the rising ground with himself as boss. Facing him was Mar's army led by dudes who went by the names McDonnell of Glengarry, MacLean of Duart and Macdonald of Clanranald.

The attack was furious the Highlanders as usual ran into the battle after releasing their plaids. The Highlanders with willy's flying all over the place attacked in the scud or with just their shirts on. Some was swinging the lethal claymore others with broadsword in one hand and targe and Dirk in the other.

They soon broke through the right wing of Mr. Argyll's troops. With one of his wings totally slaughtered and one of his main commanders doing a runner. Argyll himself led his dragoons and attacked the flank of Mar's army, driving him back a couple of miles.

Thus meaning both sides had one of their flanks defeated. Both sides were finding this little punch up no very funny, they were no longer able to punch each other's heed in.

Argyll buggered off back to Dunblane, meanwhile Mar went back to his house in Perth. The outcome of the battle was simple, there wasn't one?

The Jacobites still had the problem of Argyll blocking the way to England. Mar was holding Perth but to no avail his Highlanders were missing their haggis. They were getting fed up with the no win situation and the fact there wasn't much in the way of plunder.

They soon started to bugger off, back to their houses in the Highlands. Argyll meanwhile received his re-enforcements and now he heavily outnumbered Mar.

It was only the good old Scottish weather that stopped him having a go, he was held back by heavy snow.

This was the position when James landed on 22nd December 1715. He set foot ashore at Peterhead, but he landed to a cause that was already lost. James himself was no feeling right; he had managed to get himself some fever.

It didn't help matters that some gold given to him as a pressie from the Spaniards had been lost in the sea off Dundee. James set foot into his Kingdom but was unable to raise the spirits of his followers. He only managed to grumble that his life had been full of misfortunes from birth to present day.

By the end of January 1716 came the news that Argyll was on his way with a large group of buddies and they would like to have a wee word in his ear. Mr. Mar didn't like the sound of this so he retreated, he and James decided on a wee boat trip to Froggieland.

When the remaining Highland army reached Aberdeen a letter was read out to them on behalf of King James. The letter told them plain and simple to get on with things and look out for themselves.

In London it was decided that steps should be taken to stop the rebellious Scots from taking up arms again. Scots by the hundreds were sent to the Plantations and for good measure two of the Jacobite leaders who had failed to catch the boat were put to death.

The Clans were ordered to disarm or else, this proved only partly successful. The Clans loyal to the Hanoverian cause were nice enough to hand over their weapons. The other Clans only handed over broken and useless weapons.

The union with England was now as popular as chronic toothache at a toffee chewing convention. Even the Scots who had supported the union at first were now against it because of the Government's attitude to Scotland and her people.

The Jacobites soon found they had a mate in sunny Spain a dude who went by the name Cardinal Alberoni (nice dish that I've had it a couple of times myself). He was a chappie with a fair bit of clout in Spain. In 1719 he made a deal with his mates the Jacobites.

The deal on offer was that two frigates with 300 Spanish soldiers armed to the teeth were to come to Scotland for a wee break. They were to land on the sunny West Coast.

When they weren't being eaten alive by the midges, they were to raise the Clans.

While these chappies were doing this a force of 27 ships with 5,000 of their best buddies would make their way to England introduce themselves and then kill the locals.

This was a cunning little plan and had a good chance of succeeding, but once again the Jacobites luck was out the window. A storm broke up the main expedition before they could land.

The Spanish party landed at Loch Alsh then went for a wee stroll to Glenshiel. No being on the bright side they soon got confused with their surroundings and bumped into the much larger Government army.

They calmly thought their situation out, then said 'fuck this for a game of soldiers' then stuck their hands in the air and surrendered. The Spanish did bring a few weapons with them and 6,000 much needed muskets found their way to Jacobite hands.

The English continued in their pursuit of subjugating the Highlands. Once again one of their main aims was to get rid of what they termed the 'Irish' tongue. The order was to wear it out and the people were to learn the English tongue. Not surprisingly most folks just turned round and stuck their tongues out at this.

In 1725 a strict disarming Act was passed, the Highlanders for a time were no longer allowed to wear arms(I hope they were allowed to keep their legs!) in public. While all this was going on a dude who went by the name General Wade had been given the jobbie as Commander-in-Chief for Scotland.

He embarked on a 10-year mission to build roads for the Government forces to move about the Highlands. This would mean they could move faster to kick any heads in that were thinking about rising.

These roads were to be linked to the Government strongholds of Fort William, Fort Kilchumin and Fort George. When built these roads would cover over 260 miles and give the Government much more control over the Highlands and destroy the old way of life which still existed there.

A regiment of dudes was formed to police the Highlands, they became known as the 'Black Watch'. Talk was rife about their 'over-friendliness' toward sheep!

In 1727 George I did the time honoured thing and ate no more sausages.

He was succeeded by George II (also known as 'krautie II' to his mates), once again Scotland had a King who cared in the least not about her.

The folks of bonnie Scotland grew further from Government rule. They were no happy bunnies about new taxes being placed on them. Riots would burst out from time to time.

A fun day to be had by all, simply throw one dead cat out the window. This would let others know you were in the mood for a good riot and off you go. The hero's of the day were smugglers and the baddies of the day were the excise-men.

The people of Scotland were living in a tinderbox and in 1736 came an excuse to express their feelings. The dudes of Edinburgh especially enjoyed going on the streets and having a good time smashing things up, when they thought an injustice had been done.

The 1736 riot became known as the 'Porteous Riots.' In 1690 a dude who went by the name Johnny Porteous was born in the Cannongate of Edinburgh, he was the son of a tailor. Mr. Porteous wanted to be a tailor like his old man. His Daddy told him to take a hike as he couldn't stand his laddies violent temper.

Johnny therefore decided it would be nice to travel to foreign countries meet the locals then shoot them. So he joined the army and served in Holland, he returned to Edinburgh in 1715.

He was given the jobbie of drillmaster to the 'Town Guard.' It was the Town Guards jobbie to keep law and order. They were a much-hated lot, nearly always pissed out their skulls. The good folks of Edinburgh having full respect for those in power call the Town Guard, the 'Toun Rats.'

In 1726 Johnny boy had worked his way up the ladder and was made Captain/Lieutenant he now had a fair bit of clout, but he lacked mates.

In 1736 he was to find out just how popular he was or not as the case may be.

On 14th April he was in charge of the execution of a dude who went by the name Andy Wilson. He was a very popular chappie as his daytime or more to the point his nighttime jobbie was a smuggler.

Mr. Wilson was to be strung up with his partner a dude who went by the name Georgie Robertson. Both men were taken from the jail to St Giles for a nice little religious service, before they were hanged.

It didn't take long for Andy to notice that the Town Guard who were lining the aisle and guarding the doors, were as pissed as newts. Andy cared not for his own life he grabbed one of the drunk guards under his arm. He then grabbed another under his other arm, then shouted 'run Georgie run.' He then held a third guard back with his teeth!

Georgie as told did a runner and escaped. Porteous was as mad as a Polar Bear without any mints! He had manacles forced on to Andy. They were far too small and the blood poured from his wrists and ankles.

He was taken straight from the Church to the Grassmarket area, were he was to be hanged straight away. Porteous placed the Town Guard round the gallows. The people of Edinburgh gathered to watch the barbaric treatment of Andy. He was strung up and hanged.

Twenty minutes after he was hanged Porteous ordered that he be cut down and pronounced dead.

When Johnny big man Porteous walked out from behind his guards into the open crowd he was hit by a stone, more stones soon followed. Being a mild natured chappie he drew his pistol and opened fire on the crowd.

The Town Guard took this as a sign to open fire, 20 folks were shot. Six of them were shot so bad that they decided to stop breathing. The crowd scampered in terror.

Edinburgh was ready to erupt something had to be done. The Lord Provost a dude who went by the name Alexander Wilson had no choice but to have Johnny arrested and put on trial.

Johnny boy was found guilty by a huge majority of one, but that was enough to seal his fate. He was condemned to hang. Mr. Porteous was placed in Edinburgh's notorious jail the 'Tolbooth.'

The London Government were horrified when the news reached them. George II was on one of his many holidays to Germany and was not due back for some weeks.

So the news of Mr. Porteous was relayed to the King's wife Caroline. The Queen immediately pardoned Johnny, but he'd have to stay in jail for another six weeks till her hubby came home.

When this news broke in Edinburgh the people were spitting blood, once again England had over-ruled them. On 7th September a wee mob of over 4,000 took to the streets. They forced the laddie of the Burgh's drummer to march ahead of them beating a call to arms.

There was going to be justice at whatever cost. The crowd blocked all the gates to the town, keeping most of the Town Guard outside. Now in control of the town, they made their way to the Tollbooth.

They tried kicking the door in then they tried battering the great door, but it wouldn't budge. So they decided to burn down the door. However in order to do no more damage than necessary they had buckets of water on hand.

This riot was organised with some perfection, in fact quite a few of the women in the crowd were in fact not women but guys in women's clothing. Why there were transvestites among the rioters, the answer is simple. Among the rioters were some folks in very high jobbies who wanted justice done. They had to disguise themselves in fear of being found out and hanged.

With the door burned down the rioters entered the jail. They began to search high and low for Johnny. He being the brave chappie he was hid up the chimney, doing a Santa Claus impersonation didn't save him he was found and dragged out.

He was told what a bad chappie he was and that he was going to get his wrist slapped and to get the point over he was to be hanged as well.

Johnny was dragged to the place he had hung Andy. When the crowd of 4,000 got him to the Grassmarket they showed how organised they were, by realising not one of them had thought to bring a very vital ingredient needed for a hanging, a rope!

It was then decided to kick in the door of a near-by shop. But this was a rioting crowd whose anger was vented on Mr. Porteous and the injustices of the London Government, not a rope maker. A gold Guinea was left on the counter to pay for any damage done. The fact that payment was left once again proved that some very important dudes were involved.

Now the crowd had the rope, it was time to hang Porteous then they noticed they were missing something else. Gallows the town gallows were locked away in St Giles. So they threw the rope over a dyers pole and strung Johnny up. With Porteous hanged the crowd disappeared into the night.

When Queen Caroline heard what had happen she flipped her lid. She offered a Kings Pardon plus 200 nicker to anyone who would grass any of the rioters. Even though there was over 4,000 involved in the lynching of Johnny and a fortune in dosh offered. Not one of the rioters was ever turned in.

Queen Caroline at first wanted the City Charter to be destroyed and the Town Guard to be disbanded. The gates to the city were to be demolished and the Provost to be chucked in the clink. It was only after the intervention of Argyll that she was stopped in her tracks and instead imposed a huge fine on the city.

Needless to say all this did nothing to endear the House of Hanover to their Scottish subjects.

Meanwhile Europe was on the edge of war. It wasn't long before

Britain was at war with Spain and France. The Jacobites once more had hopes of another uprising, by this time the Jacobites had a new card they could play.

A dude who went by the name Prince Charles Edward Stewart (also known as 'Doughnut Brain' to his mates), he was the elder laddie of King James VIII & III. Bonnie Prince Charlie as he became known was born in Rome in 1720.

He had much more spunk than his old man. He was a fit young chappie who had personal magnetism and what's more he was more than willing to punch faces in for his Daddy's throne. In January 1744 Charlie left Rome and set off to France.

His timing was spot on as the French were planning a wee trip over the English Channel to do some duty free shopping and invade England while they were at it. The Frogs had formed a large invasion force, which was assembled at Dunkirk. The storms of March that year put paid to their plans.

The following year the Froggie's kicked the shit out of the English at Fontenoy. Charlie's hopes were once more raised. He didn't quite get the support he was hoping for and was going to have to get the ball rolling by himself.

So he raised some dosh by pawning his mummy's rubies. He used the cash to fit out a frigate, the 'Doutelle.' He also fitted out a ship called the 'Elizabeth.' In July he and they would set sail for bonnie Scotland from Nantes.

Set sail they did right into the path of an English warship, the 'Elizabeth' took a doing and had to return to France. The 'Doutelle' escaped and on 2nd of August Charlie and seven of his buddies landed on the Island of Eriskay.

The reception that greeted him was hardy overwhelming. He was met by two dudes who went by the names Macleod and Macdonald of Sleat. Both these chappies in the past had been very loyal to the House of Stuart. But they both now thought the cause was lost.

They politely told him do yourself a favour and go home. Charles replied in his strong eyetie accent 'I am come home.' Charlie and his seven buddies then set sail once more this time to a joint called Moidart.

On landing there Charlie soon found he had a new buddy, a dude who went by the name Macdonald of Clanranald, he at once rallied to the bonnie Prince. Charlie and his mates became known as the 'seven men of Moidart' even though there was in fact nine of them.

These dudes went by the names Willie Murray, Marquess of Tullibardine. Sir Tam Sheridan the chappie who used to teach Charlie. Sir Johnny Macdonald an officer in the French service. Colonel John O'Sullivan a dodgy Irish soldier of fortune. Francis Strickland an English Jacobite. Geogie Kelly a nonjuring man of the cloth. Aeneas Macdonald a Paris banker and brother to Macdonald of Kinloch Moidart.

Charlie and his mates brought some implements with them that they thought would come in handy. One thousand muskets and 1800 broadswords, and a few small field pieces, plus 4000 Louis D'Or.

He was soon joined by a dude who went by the name Donald Cameron he held the jobbie of 19th Chief of the Clan Cameron. He became known as the 'Gentle Lochiel'.

His family more than anything wanted the House of Stuart back on the throne. He however was not sure if the time was right for Charlie to get the backing he needed.

Lochiel met Charlie for a pint and shook hands with him and decided he wasn't a bad dude so he swore to help him.

Within a few days he left with the other Chiefs to raise the Highland Clans for Charlie.

Plans were now afoot to raise the Royal Standard at Glenfinnan. This joint was chosen because of its location in the heart of the Glens as well as the fact it happen to be in the middle of Macdonald and Cameron country. Word soon got about that the Standard was being raised.

Charlie having sent the 'Doutelle' back to France set up his headquarters at Kinloch Moidart. It was here another mate a dude who went by the name Johnny Murray of Broughton joined him. He took on the jobbie as Charlie's secretary.

On 18th August they moved again this time to Loch Shiel then up the Loch to Glenaladale. It was here that a dude who went by the name Gordon of Glenbucket joined them. He brought with him a wee pressie for Charlie. An English officer, who went by the name Captain Swettenham, this guy, had been silly enough to get himself captured by the Macdonald's.

On the morning 19th August guarded by 50 Macdonald's, the seven dudes of Moidart and a few mates who had rose to the call rowed up the Loch with Charlie to Glenfinnan. It was a crappy sort of day with the usual rain and fog, other words a typical summer's day in the Highlands.

This small band of men gathered together. To greet them there was a handful of nosy buggers. Before long Macdonald of Morar joined them, he brought with him a 150 of his buddies.

The wait was on to see who else would rise, in the afternoon. What sounded like a cat that had just been stood on turned out to be the skirl of the pipes. They were heard coming over the hills. It was Lochiel with him he brought 700 of his mates as well as a party of redcoats to boot Government soldiers who had been captured.

Soon more Highlanders appeared; Charlie's mob was growing it was now numbering about 1400 give or take one or two that is.

The Marquess of Tullibardine unfurled the Royal Standard and read out King James' proclamation. This stated that Charlie had been given the jobbie as Regent. The bonnie Prince got on his soapbox and gibbered what is best described as a short pathetic speech.

After he finished gibbering Charlie turned to Captain Swettenham and told him to fuck off and tell his General what he had seen on this day. He was also to tell his boss that Charlie and his sidekicks were on the way to give him a good kicking!

With the Standard of cloth, white, blue and red fluttering above Charlie and his Highlanders were ready to kick butt.

He began his hike to Edinburgh picking up more helpers on the way, before long he had a following of 3000! The news of what was happening soon reached the ears of a dude who went by the name General Sir Johnny Cope, he was an English chappie and his daytime jobbie was Commander-in-Chief of the Government forces.

He got out of the way of Charlie's troops and withdrew northwards towards Inverness, leaving the road clear for Edinburgh. Charlie liked Perth so he took it then moved onwards.

At Coltbridge they bumped into a couple of Government dragoons gave them a kicking and moved on.

Edinburgh soon got word the Jacobites were on their way. The town handled it with suave decorum and panicked. The Town Guard handled the situation by doing a runner.

Charlie and his chappies reached the town wall and settled outside. Over a couple beers they tried to figure out the best way of taking the town. Getting over the wall could prove to be difficult.

Getting in to the town was to prove a piece of cake; a group of Cameron's noticed the Netherbow Port gate opening to let a coach out. They put their trainers on and rushed the gate and secured it open, the Jacobites entered the City of Edinburgh.

At the Mercat Cross the following day King James VIII & III was proclaimed King.

Charles who was now chuffed to pieces entered The Palace of Holyrood. The folks of Edinburgh took to Charlie and his mates right away and cheered them all the way.

Mr. Cope was at this time enjoying the sights of Aberdeen. He was trying to cope the best he could. He was also hoping Clans like the Fraser's would come to his aid.

He soon found out these chappies were not going to rush to him, but was waiting to see how things processed.

Mr. Cope soon realised he could soon be up to his neck in obnoxious odours. So he placed all his troops on ships and landed them at Dunbar. From there he took his guys on a wee hike towards Edinburgh. He camped his men at the village of Prestonpans, just a few miles from Edinburgh.

On hearing this news Charlie and his chums left Edinburgh and made their way to meet Mr. Cope they had plans to stick the heed on him. Johnny Cope being the clever General he was come to the conclusion that the Jacobites would attack from the west and therefore drew is army up at Prestonpans.

He settled in and waited for reinforcements who were making their way from Berwick.

Charlie's Commander a dude who went by the name Lord George Murray was no daft cookie. He took his Jacobite troops a nice long walk circling round to the south. This allowed Mr. Murray to launch his attack from the east and taking Mr. Cope up the rear to his total surprise!

The charge was launched about 2am in the morning. It had come to Jacobite ears that before they arrived the Government Forces were rife with rumours. It was believed the Jacobite army was filled with nasty big hairy dudes who all carried Claymores. What's more they could take a mans head off with one swipe. Once the head was removed they would then eat it for lunch!

Murray played the Government at their own propaganda game. He ordered his chappies to scream 'Claymore, Claymore' as they run into the punch up. The English shit themselves; the battle was over in less than 15 minutes.

The Government forces took to their heels and done a runner. Mr. Cope's infantry had no hope against the Highland charge. Johnny Cope leaving what was left of his troops to stick their hands up, while he did a runner with his two regiments of dragoons.

Cope didn't stop riding his horse, even beating the advance party till he reached Berwick. It is said he was the first General in all Europe to bring news of his own defeat!

Winning the battle of Prestonpans was good news for Charlie and the Jacobites, as it meant they were now in control of bonnie Scotland. London was fast going into a state of panic. Charlie should have took full advantage of his victory and carried on with his advance.

Instead he stayed in Edinburgh for another four weeks, holding grand balls in Holyrood Palace. King Georgie having wet his pants brought as many troops as he could back from Flanders. He sent them packing to meet up with General Wade. Who was in fact no longer a General but now held the jobbie as Field Marshal, he was staying at Newcastle.

While all this was going on in London a new verse was added on to the National Anthem and was sung nightly at Dury Lane to a standing ovation.

> GOD GRANT THAT MARSHAL WADE,
> MAY BY THY MIGHTY AID VICTORY BRING,
> MAY HE SEDITION HUSH,
> AND LIKE A TORRENT RUSH,
> REBELLIOUS SCOTS TO CRUSH,
> GOD SAVE THE KING

Charlie all the while was hoping for support from his Froggie mates. He got dosh and some supplies but no men. By his own account Charlie reckoned he had an army of 8,000 with 300 horses.

In November he decided to take his chappies for a wee holiday over the Border. Charlie wanted to go straight to Newcastle and beat up the ageing Mr. Wade. Mr. Murray told him it's no very nice to go about beating up pensioners. It was therefore decided to move up into Lancashire there it was hoped they would meet up with large numbers of English

Jacobites. This however was not to be. On this little hike the Jacobites met with no real resistance.

The people of England were relieved to find out the Highlanders were not savages and cannibals as they had been led to believe.

The only sizeable force of Jacobites to join Charlie came from Manchester and numbered about 300. The Jacobite army didn't get the new recruits as hoped for. Even worse they were starting to lose some of their dudes. Some of the homesick Highlanders started to desert home. Coffin-dodger Wade was now threatening Charlie's army from the north-east. Another Government army was advancing from the Midlands; this one was led by George II's fat laddie a dude who went by the name Duke of Cumberland (also known as 'Sicko' to his mates).

Charlie was now facing the wrath of about 30,000 pissed off English troops, against his badly equipped 5,000. At the beginning of December the Highlanders had reached Derby.

Charlie and his leaders had a wee chat and tried to work a way out of the deep shit they were now in. He knew he was only 130 miles from London and had not kicked butt once. Unbeknown to Charlie London was in a total state of fear and panic.

The Bank of England was paying out in sixpences and Georgie had all his gear and treasures loaded on to ships in the Thames. He was ready to do a runner over to Hanover.

If Charlie had moved there and then to London he may have been successful and the Jacobite cause may well have been won, but he and they did not.

Mr. Murray and his advisors knew full well that they could never hold London. Of course they had no idea the good folks of London were shitting themselves, so they advised that Charlie turn his mates round and head back to Scotland.

The plan was to return to the Highlands and launch a new campaign in the spring.

Charlie was starting to find comfort in the bottle. On 6th December 1745 the Jacobites having enjoyed their wee break in England started their hike home. Thirteen days later they were back on Scottish soil, but not everyone was overly friendly to have them on home soil.

Dumfries was very rude to them to say the least and Glasgow wasn't all that much nicer. In the Highlands the Clans once more came to their Prince's aid. Not all a few joined the Hanoverian cause. Clans such as the Sutherlands, Macleod's MacKay's and Munroe's were all firmly on the side of the House of Hanover.

Lord Lovat however made up his mind that there might be a Jacobite Dukedom coming his way therefore put his Fraser's on the side of Charlie.

In January 1746 Charlie once more had a force of 8,000. At the joint called Falkirk he met an English dude who went by the name General Hawley who just happened to have with him a much larger army of

Government troops.

Mr. Hawley didn't expect to bump into the Jacobites. When his scouts brought him the news that the Jacobites were just over the hill on high ground, Hawley in a mad rush ordered his guy's forward. They ran up the hill towards the Jacobites the rain was pissing down. In the confusion that followed there was a punch up in the fog and on boggy ground.

The scrap only lasted 20 minutes.

The Highlanders were in no mood to play games in this foul weather, so they quickly slaughtered hundreds of Hawley's chappies. The Jacobites losses numbered less than 50.

Mr. Hawley said, 'oh fuck', and did a runner with his chappies back to Linithgow. The Jacobites gave themselves a pat on the back and returned to Stirling.

Charlie didn't follow up his advantage and moved his guy's up north to Inverness.

During this time the 'Rout of Moy' occurred. Lord Loudon Redcoat boss of the North heard Charlie was staying with infamous bird, Lady 'Colonel' Annie Mackintosh.

Under the cover of darkness Loudon and 1500 of his mates decided to capture Charlie.

However a warning had reached Charlie's lugs that they were approaching. Charlie did a runner in his nightshirt. To avoid pursuit Lady Annie came up with a cunning plan.

She sent six of her servants including the local blacksmith with muskets. These six dudes were to ambush Loudon's small group of 1500! They placed their muskets at intervals on a ridge above the approaching column. When they seen the army in front, these six chappies started to run backward and forwards, pretending to be Clan Chiefs. They were screaming things like Mackintosh's forward, Cameron's forward. The Government forces shit themselves on the spot. They thought they had walked right into a Jacobite ambush!

They turned their heels and buggered off quick-style. Six men fooled 1500 and Charlie made his way safely to Inverness.

He made his headquarters in the town. The moral of his men was beginning to run low. They began to wander back to their homes to check their love ones.

Charlie then heard the charming news that fat boy Cumberland was heading north with an army at least double the size of the Jacobite army. What's more the Government army was well fed, well trained, and well armed.

Mr. Cumberland had spent six weeks in Aberdeen receiving more troops from Flanders.

He spent the time carefully preparing them. He was now heading towards Inverness to kick Charlie's arse.

Charles had to get his army together and that was no easy task. He got together about 5,000 hungry and ill equipped guys. Mr. Murray urged

Charlie to withdraw his men into the hills and fight a guerrilla war. By now Charlie was beginning to lose the plot, he didn't have any trust in his Commander and started to take the advice of his drinking buddy Colonel Johnny boy O'Sullivan.

Charlie took the advice of the clown O'Sullivan to have a battle with the Government forces on open field.

Drummossie Moor near Culloden was chosen. This field was totally useless to the Highlander's; it was flat as a pancake! The Highland charge was always led downhill a feat that was impossible on Drummossie Moor.

Charlie heard Mr. Cumberland's troops were camped 11 miles away at the seaside resort of Nairn it was also his fat cousin's birthday. Charlie worked out that Mr. Cumberland's buddies would be on the piss to celebrate his birthday. So Charlie decided to take his chappies on a wee hike to sing 'happy birthday to you.' Then for a birthday pressie run a sword through him.

His night attack plan was a total failure and he only achieved in knackering his men for the forthcoming punch up.

On 16th April 1746 a sleepless unfed and poorly equipped Jacobite army faced a larger well rested, well fed and most of all well armed Government army. This scrap wasn't looking good for Charlie and his mates.

The Jacobites were poorly positioned and were soon cut to pieces by the Government's grapeshot (Oh I'm so angry I could crush a grape!). Within 20 minutes of the barrage the Jacobites were restless, and wanted to get tore in. The charge was called but the boggy ground greatly hindered their attack.

One group amazingly managed to break through the Hanoverian line, but at a high cost in casualties. Those who broke through to kick butt were soon cut down by the deadly fusillades from the regiment behind.

Mr. Cumberland's cavalry finished off the rout. The battle was over in 45 minutes, 1500 men lay spattered on Drummossie Moor, most of them Jacobites. Cumberland won a battle he could never lose. The Duke considered the Jacobite savages after the fight he left the wounded Jacobites lying on the field to die in the rain.

Some were piled on top of each other and the cannons were fired into them. Hundreds of Jacobite wounded, were on Cumberland's orders shot were they lay or if it be more convenient burned alive, so as not to waste any more powder.

Those who were still alive over the next couple of days were bayoneted to death.

Before the punch up Cumberland lied to his guy's and told them that he had seen the Jacobite orders and no quarter was to be given by them.

It was in fact he that gave no quarter. When the battle was lost Charlie was led from the field with tears in his eyes. The last words it's claimed he heard as he was leaving the field were those of Lord Elcho 'There you go for a damned cowardly Italian.'

After the battle of Culloden, Mr Cumberland showed his hate for the

Highlanders. The reprisals were horrific. Government troops were sent into the hills they were given orders by Cumberland to hunt down the fugitives like dogs. Houses were looted and burned to the ground, cattle were driven away and the crops were destroyed.

The town of Inverness was to suffer terribly. It was there that Mr. Cumberland committed one of his worst crimes. After the battle amazingly a large group of Jacobites escaped the field and made their way to the town.

When they reached it they came face to face with Campbell Militia. They were too knackered to swim the river that was on high tide, so they were simply rounded up.

They were taken to the High Kirk graveyard, to be kept prisoner. They slept were they fell. It was 12 hours before Cumberland got word that this large group of Jacobites had been captured. He simply said dispose of them and remember enough powder has been wasted.

They were all put to death were they lay. Right after they were murdered Lord Lovat's cattle was impounded and taken to the Kirk yard. This of course covered up the crime that had been committed there.

In the town itself the 'Redcoat's' bayonet became known as the 'baby-jabber' as Redcoat soldiers were seen running through the town with babies hanging from their bayonets.

The Provost of Inverness himself a Hanoverian supporter went to Cumberland to beg for some leniency in the treatment of his people. He was kicked down the stairs by one of Cumberland's officers. The aftermath of the Battle of Culloden is estimated to be between 15,000 and 30,000.

Charlie himself went into hiding he was a wanted man with a lot of dosh on his head, £30,000. He wandered about the Highlands and Islands for five long months.

It was known by many were he was but no one would turn him in despite the fortune that was on offer.

Government forces swarmed the Highlands destroying everything they could while hunting for Charlie. On 19th September 1746, with some difficulty Charlie was picked up by a French frigate from the shores of the same Loch he 'had come home' 14 months before.

For the chappie who once said, 'I am come home' it was time for him to go home. He was taken back to France, leaving a broken and destroyed country.

Charlie spent the rest of his life a sour-faced piss-artist; he stuffed it in Rome in 1788.

Cumberland went back to London; there he was made a hero. The English named a flower after him 'sweet William', the Scots named a weed after him 'Stinking Billy'. A hero he was to some, but his old man the King was never to speak to him again. George II never forgave him for his savage treatment of the Scots.

He earned his name in history as 'Butcher Cumberland.' After the slaughter of Culloden the Government brought in a series of Acts to make sure there was never another Jacobite uprising and to destroy the sprits and the way of life in the Highlands. The destruction was total.

The Episcopal Church, which it was believed to have shown support to the Jacobite cause, had its arse well and truly kicked. Jacobite followers were rounded up and executed.

In 1747 Lord Lovat became the last peer to be publicly beheaded.

Lovat the head of the Clan Fraser was known as the 'Sly Fox', he had swapped sides many times in his long career. He opted for the Jacobite cause when they looked so close to winning. He was taken to the 'Tower of London.' There he was to be beheaded by this time he cared not he was 80 years old.

When all his enemies heard he was going to get his head cut off, they all demanded to be at the beheading. Seating was built so they could all come and view Lovat losing his heed. He knew nothing of this and when he went out on his day of execution, he was very bemused to see them all sitting there.

He turned round in his broad Scots and said 'What are a' that lot gawking at, ha'I'v nthin better t' dae than see an old man wi' grey hair aboot t' get his heed cut off!', he cared not.

His head was placed on the block, as the axe hit it all his enemies jumped up and cheered. The seating collapsed and about fifty of them were killed! Lord Lovat had the last laugh and that's where the phrase 'Laughing yer head off' comes from.

Hundreds of Clansmen were sent over to the plantations. The Jacobite Chiefs all had their lands taken from them. Then one of the worst Acts a Government ever imposed on its own subjects was brought out. The 'Disarming Act, 1746' this Act forbid the wearing of weapons, the wearing of tartan even the playing of the fiddle was banned. In fact anything Scottish was outlawed one poor chappie was hanged for playing the pipes.

The Government's main policy was to rid the Scots from their own land and send them overseas. Horrific as the measures were the Scots spirits were not broken and English spies reported that some were still more than willing to rise again, if help could be sought from France.

In 1752 a dude who went by the name Campbell of Glenure was engaged in the Government's dirty work of evicting tenants from the well-protected lands of Lochiel and of Ardshiel in Appin. He was a much-hated figure and he was shot very much dead in broad daylight by a sniper who had planned his attack very well.

The sniper got clean away. The Duke of Argyll went nuts, so to make an example he had an innocent man hanged. The Highlands of Scotland would never again be able to rise.

On Charlie's death in 1788 his wee brother succeeded him. He was a dude who went by the name Henry. He kicked the bucket in 1807 and with him died the House of Stuart.

12 years after he keeled over a distant relative the 'heedbanger', King George III (also known as 'Srewball' to his mates) who had come to the

throne in 1760 paid for a fine marble tomb. This was erected over the two brothers and their Daddy.

George III died a madman in 1820; he was succeeded by his laddie, George IV (also known as 'Twat' to his mates). With the Stuart line no more and the Highlands tamed, Georgie boy decided to visit Scotland.

He had been talked into the visit by the great but foolish Sir Walter Scott. He was to be the first monarch of Scotland to visit Scotland in 172 years! For the visit Scott reinvented Scottish history as well as the Highland dress.

The King landed at Leith wearing what he was led to believe was Royal Stuart tartan, while Scott himself wore Campbell tartan.

Many pissed themselves laughing at the Kings flesh covered tights, which he wore under his kilt. The tights were needed to cover his pox-covered legs!

Scotland became the in place to be with George IV's niece Queen Victoria (also known as 'Ugly Git' to her mates). She fell in love with Scotland, but she fell in love with a Scotland that now existed and not the Scotland that once existed.

After the horrors of the aftermath of the '45 Scotland was to suffer one more horrific and shameful deed.

'The Clearances' between 1785 and 1850, the Highlands and Islands were to witness large-scale clearances. People were removed from their lands and many were sent overseas.

It had been decided that the lands were more profitable with sheep on them. The land owning rich were given an excuse as well as a way to support their lifestyles. They had already upped their rents as much as they could, causing great hardships for the working poor.

Soon incoming sheep farmers started to offer crazy amounts of dosh for land for their sheep. This caused large areas to be cleared of people to make sheep runs. These were the 'Highland Clearances.' The people were herded off their lands often at a moment's notice.

They were placed on poor land in shocking conditions of great poverty.

The Gaelic way of life was all but gone; an English-only policy was forced on the ordinary people. Who were conditioned to believe that the Highland way of life and the Gaelic tongue were a mark of ignorance, were-as English was that of success and progress.

The war overseas in Canada was London's opportunity to recruit Highlander's for military service. The reason was simple in the Government's own words 'no mischief if they should fall.'

THIS BOOK IS TO BE TAKEN AS A PIECE OF FUN. I HAVE SET OUT TO LET SOME OF SCOTLAND'S AMAZING HERITAGE BE KNOWN. I WAS ASKED BY MANY VISITORS FROM OVERSEAS AND OVER THE WALL, TO WRITE A BOOK ON SCOTLAND'S HISTORY AND ITS CHARACTERS.

THIS BOOK HAS BEEN WRITTEN AS ASKED! I HAVE INCLUDED THE PARTS OF SCOTLAND'S PAST THAT MOST PEOPLE WANT TO KNOW ABOUT, WHILE AT THE SAME TIME KEEPING THE HUMOUR GOING. I HAVE WRITTEN THE BOOK EXACTLY THE WAY I TELL THE STORIES.

I HOPE BY WRITING IN WHAT CAN ONLY BE CLASSED AS A CRINGEABLE MANNER, IT WILL ACHIEVE TWO THINGS, FIRSTLY TO BE ENJOYABLE TO READ, SECONDLY TO TRY AND EDUCATE.

MOST OF ALL NO OFFENCE IS MEANT TO ANY PERSON LIVING OR DEAD, NO OFFENCE IS MEANT TO ANY COUNTRY OR PLACE OR ITS CITIZENS. IN FACT NO OFFENCE IS MEANT TO ANYONE OR ANYTHING (EXCEPT MY WIFE!). MORE THAN ANYTHING ELSE I HOPE THIS BOOK HAS PROVED INTERESTING AND ENTERTAINING. I WOULD LIKE TO END THIS BOOK WITH THAT OLD SCOTTISH TOAST!

> *HERE'S T' YOU, AN' HERE'S T' ME,*
> *LET'S HOPE WE NEVER, DISAGREE,*
> *BUT IF WE DO, DISAGREE.*
> *HERE'S T' ME, AND T' FUCK WITH YOU!*

Davy the Ghost

To be continued with Day 3 and Day 4 ...

Glossary of Terms for Davytheghost

- **Nut**   –   head
- **Grub**   –   food
- **Yaks'**   –   eyes
- **Digs**   –   living quarters
- **Porkies**   –   lies
- **Geezer**   –   male
- **Jobbie**   –   job/employment
- **Nutter**   –   crazy person
- **I'll nut you**   –   to head-butt
- **Beastie**   –   Scots term for insects/animals
- **Ticking off**   –   row
- **Dab hand**   –   experienced
- **Dram**   –   Scottish term for a glass of a spirit
- **Laddie**   –   young male
- **Wee**   –   small
- **Croaked it**   –   died
- **Bad eggs**   –   bad persons
- **Done in**   –   to be caused physical injury/death
- **Crapped themselves**   –   got a fright
- **Get stuffed**   –   to dismiss an idea
- **Loot**   –   belongings intended to be taken/stolen
- **Dosh**   –   money
- **Gits**   –   unlikeable persons
- **Dished out**   –   to be given
- **Get togethers'**   –   gatherings/meetings
- **Nicked gear**   –   stolen goods
- **Punch up**   –   fight
- **Copped his lot**   –   died
- **Hitched**   –   married
- **Gibber on**   –   to continue monotonously
- **Chuffed with himself**   –   pleased/satisfied with oneself
- **Chin-wag**   –   conversation
- **Been stuffed**   –   beaten/defeated
- **Nuts**   –   testicles
- **Nicked**   –   stolen, taken without permission
- **Wee lass**   –   young girl
- **Got his claws into**   –   got involved with
- **Out the window**   –   dismissed
- **Rough Diamond**   –   rough and ready but with a heart of gold
- **Poofter**   –   homosexual
- **Religious nut**   –   dedicated person of religion
- **Gob**   –   mouth
- **Fibs**   –   lies
- **Hubby**   –   husband

- **Was no more** – deceased. no longer alive
- **Daft** – stupid
- **Hit the big snooze button** – to die
- **Clued up** – to be well informed
- **Fannying about** – no messing around
- **Snuffed it** – died
- **In the thick of it** – in trouble
- **Had a bee in his bonnet** – obsessed/determined/persistant
- **Puss** – face
- **The nick** – prison
- **Quick off the mark** – fast
- **Missus** – wife
- **Kicked the bucket** – died
- **Crotched it** – died
- **Keeled over** – to fall/die
- **Got knotted** – to get married
- **Copped her lot** – died
- **Seeing eye to eye** – having similar views
- **A breather** – a break/time out
- **Nookie** – aspects of sex
- **Choppy water** – not calm
- **Up the kite** – pregnant/with child
- **Porky pies** – lies
- **Buddies** – acquaintances/friends
- **Kneb** – nose
- **Chancer** – opportunist
- **Lost the plot** – to have gone crazy
- **Showing true colours** – to show one's true character
- **Scrap** – physical fight
- **Walk all over them** – to take advantage
- **Bird** – female/girlfriend
- **Crapping himself** – scared/anxious
- **Coffin dodger** – avoider of death
- **Mugs** – persons of naivity
- **Gub** – mouth
- **Wasters** – worthless irrelevant persons
- **Chin wag** – conversation
- **Done a runner** – to leave/escape
- **Pongy** – to smell bad
- **Snuffed it** – died
- **Going bananas** – to be unhappy, frantic
- **Bottle** – confidence
- **Within a whisker** – close
- **Loaded** – weathly
- **Dosh** – money
- **Cock-up** – mistake
- **Chums** – friends

118

• Muck up	–	mistake/mess
• Snuff it	–	to die
• Lugs	–	ears
• Cuppa	–	cup of tea/coffee
• Do him in	–	cause him physical injury
• Mush	–	face
• Hacked off	–	unimpressed
• Skint	–	lacking money
• Coupon	–	face
• Old man	–	father
• Bun in the oven	–	pregnant
• Square go	–	one on one fight
• Pad	–	living quarters
• Crash out	–	fall asleep
• Grub	–	food
• Hooter	–	nose
• Bairns	–	children
• Hoots	–	hots/attracted to
• Get shot	–	to get rid of
• Gear	–	equipment/weapons
• Nicked	–	stolen
• Boozer	–	public house
• Popped his clogs	–	to die
• Throw in the towel	–	give up
• Puking	–	to regurgitate
• Lanky	–	tall with slim build
• Din-dins	–	dinner/evening meal
• Up the stick	–	pregnant/with child
• Horse's hoof	–	rhyming slang for 'poof' – homosexual
• Big style	–	in a big way
• Bent	–	homosexual
• Gift of the gab	–	capable of charming/influential conversation
• Braw	–	fine/good
• Canty	–	very nasty
• Kip	–	to sleep
• Grub	–	food
• Nosh	–	food
• Hardy	–	strong – physically and mentally
• Popped their clogs	–	to die
• Toffs	–	snobbish persons
• Lynched	–	illegally hanged
• Claws	–	hands
• Hiding	–	to be caused physical harm
• Scud	–	in the nude